NEW YORK REVIEW BOOKS
CLASSICS

A TIME TO KEEP SILENCE

PATRICK LEIGH FERMOR was born in 1915 of English and Irish descent. After his stormy school days, followed by the walk across Europe to Constantinople that begins in *A Time of Gifts* (1977) and continues through *Between the Woods and the Water* (1986), he lived and traveled in the Balkans and the Greek archipelago. His books *Mani* (1958) and *Roumeli* (1966) attest to his deep interest in languages and remote places. In the Second World War he joined the Irish Guards, became a liaison officer in Albania, and fought in Greece and Crete. He was awarded the DSO and OBE. He now lives partly in Greece—in the house he designed with his wife, Joan, in an olive grove in the Mani—and partly in Worcestershire. He was knighted in 2004 for his services to literature and to British–Greek relations.

KAREN ARMSTRONG, a historian of religion, spent seven years in a Roman Catholic religious order; she has written about this experience in *Through the Narrow Gate* and *The Spiral Staircase*. She is also the author of many books, including *A History of God*, *The Great Transformation*, and, most recently, *The Bible: A Biography*.

Other books by Patrick Leigh Fermor published by
New York Review Books

A Time of Gifts
Between the Woods and the Water
Mani
Roumeli

A TIME TO KEEP SILENCE

PATRICK LEIGH FERMOR

Introduction by
KAREN ARMSTRONG

Drawings by
JOHN CRAXTON

NEW YORK REVIEW BOOKS

New York

THIS IS A NEW YORK REVIEW BOOK
PUBLISHED BY THE NEW YORK REVIEW OF BOOKS
435 Hudson Street, New York, NY 10014
www.nyrb.com

Published by arrangement with John Murry, Ltd.

Library of Congress Cataloging-in-Publication Data

Fermor, Patrick Leigh.
  A time to keep silence / by Patrick Leigh Fermor ; introduction by Karen
Armstrong.
      p. cm. — (New York review books classics)
  Originally published: London : Queen Anne Press, 1953.
  ISBN-13: 978-1-59017-244-5 (alk. paper)
  ISBN-10: 1-59017-244-2 (alk. paper)
  1. Monastic and religious life. 2. Monasticism and religious orders. I. Title.
BX2435.F43 2007
271.0092—dc22

                                                            2007029769

ISBN 978-1-59017-244-5

Printed in the United States of America on acid-free paper.
10 9 8 7 6 5

CONTENTS

INTRODUCTION

WHEN Patrick Leigh Fermor walked up the hill to the Abbey of St. Wandrille de Fontanelle in northern France seeking a quiet, cheap place in which to write, he entered a territory that was alien in a different way from the remote places he had described in his other travel books. Indeed, as he soon discovered, the monastery represented another world, one that entirely and deliberately reversed the norms of secular life. I had a similar experience when I entered a convent as a young girl. To an outsider, the life of monks and nuns seems forbidding and even perverse, but for centuries it has exerted an irresistible appeal, not only in Western Christendom but in almost all cultures and religious traditions.

The monastic life is so at odds with the outside world that it often inspires immense hostility. As Leigh Fermor notes repeatedly, the ruined buildings of the great abbeys and convents of Europe recall the savagery of the kings and reformers who so repeatedly razed them to the ground. Even today, people often feel affronted by the lifestyle of monks and nuns, which challenges so many of our more secular values and seems inhuman, inhumane, and joyless. Instead of seeking wealth, comfort, and material success, monks opt for poverty and do not even own their own toothbrushes. Their voluntary celibacy and renunciation of intimacy seem to violate basic human instincts in a world that lays such emphasis on family values. And, hardest of all, perhaps—though this is something Leigh Fermor does not explore—they give up their freedom and personal autonomy, vowing obedience to their superiors in a way that is repugnant to the independent ethos of modernity. And yet people continue to choose this austerity. As Leigh Fermor shows, even though their abbeys were destroyed again and again, the orders always came back and resumed the disciplines that brought the monks a peace and fulfillment that they could not find in the outside world.

Monasticism tells us something important about the structure of our humanity. Almost every single one of the major world traditions has developed some form of coenobitic life. Just as some people—at all times and in all cultures—have felt impelled to become dancers, poets, or musicians, others are irresistibly drawn to a life of silence and prayer. They have an unusual talent, by no means granted to all the faithful, for meditation, and they will never be satisfied unless they are able to develop and practice it assiduously. The athlete and the dancer reveal the potential of the human body; they willingly subject themselves to a painful, rigorous, and exhausting discipline, giving up many comforts and pleasures in order to learn their craft. Because of this dedication, they are able to perform physical feats that are beyond the reach of an untrained person. In the same way, the contemplative gladly submits to an equally demanding regimen and, once he or she has become adept, manifests the full potential of the human spirit.

It is significant that the monastic life follows a similar pattern all the world over. People have found, by trial and error, that certain practices are efficacious and that others are not. The monks' monotonous way of life has been deliberately designed to protect them from the distractions of, and the lust for, novelty: they do the same things day after day; they dress alike and shun individuality and personal style. They keep almost perpetual silence, so that their attention is directed within. They chant their scriptures together, so that the sacred texts become a part of their inner landscape. Community life is very important because the experience of living with people whom they have not chosen and may not find congenial gradually erases the selfishness that will prevent them from attaining the transcendent experience they seek.

The monastic life demands a kind of death—the death of the ego that we feed so voraciously in secular life. We are, perhaps, biologically programmed to self-preservation. Even when our physical survival is not in jeopardy, we seek to promote ourselves, to make ourselves liked, loved, and admired; display ourselves to best advantage; and pursue our own interests—often ruthlessly. But this self-preoccupation, all the world religions tell us, paradoxically holds us back from our best selves. Many of our problems spring from thwarted egotism. We resent the success of others; in our gloomiest, most self-pitying moments, we feel uniquely mistreated and undervalued; we are miserably aware of our shortcomings. In the world outside the cloister, it is always possible to escape such self-dissatisfaction: we can phone a friend, pour a drink, or turn on the television. But the religious has to face his or her pettiness twenty-four hours a day, three hundred and sixty-five days a year. If properly and wholeheartedly pursued, the monastic life liberates us from ourselves—incrementally, slowly, and imperceptibly. Once a monk has transcended his ego, he will experience an alternative mode of being. It is an *ekstasis,* a "stepping outside" the confines of self.

The ascetics of India have pursued the same goal and their way of life is remarkably similar to that of Christian monks. They designed the disciplines of yoga, for example, precisely to take the "I" out of their thinking. They thus acquired a new vision, finding that once it was no longer regarded self-referentially, even the humblest object revealed a numinous quality. Yogins train themselves to do the opposite of what comes naturally: they learn to sit without the motion that is a sign of life, as though they were statues or plants; they control their respiration, the most reflexive of our bodily functions; and they learn to curb the stream of restless thoughts that ceaselessly invade the human mind. When they have transcended the condition of normal, secular consciousness, they experience—the texts tell us—the indescribable joy and liberation of Nirvana. A Christian monk might say that they come into the presence of God.

Christian monasticism demands a similar reversal of fundamental human instincts and expectations. On his very first evening, Leigh Fermor became acutely aware of the "staggering difference" between life in the abbey and the world outside. "The thoughts, ambitions, sounds, light, time and mood that surround the inhabitants of a cloister are not only unlike anything to which one is accustomed, but in some curious way, seem its exact reverse. The period during which normal standards recede and the strange new world becomes reality is slow, and, at first, acutely painful." But after a while, when he had become accustomed to the monastic norms, Leigh Fermor found that he began to feel an unfamiliar lightness and liberty.

As he watched the monks going about their daily lives, Leigh Fermor assumed that "the dominating factor of monastic existence is a belief in the necessity and efficacy of prayer" and concluded that without "this first postulate of belief" monastic life would be farcical and intolerable. I think that he was mistaken in this. It is only since the eighteenth-century Enlightenment that the Christian West made "belief"—the acceptance of certain creedal propositions—"the first postulate" of religious life. In the West, we have developed a culture that is rational, scientific, and pragmatic; we feel obliged to satisfy ourselves that a proposition is true before we base our lives upon it, and to establish a principle to our satisfaction before we apply it. In the premodern period, however, in all the major world faiths, the main emphasis was not on belief but on behavior. First, you changed your lifestyle and only then could you experience God, Nirvana, Brahman, or the Dao as a living reality.

This has been the experience of monks and nuns. It is not belief but the disciplines of the monastic life that produce in practitioners what Christians call "faith," an apprehension of the transcendent reality of God. Doubtless, the monks that Leigh Fermor met did accept the essential doctrines of the Church and were convinced that their prayer was efficacious. But, even though he did not share these beliefs, Leigh Fermor discovered that the monastic regime changed him. When he first arrived in the abbey, he felt deeply depressed by his strange surroundings and could not sleep in his cell. But after a painful period of adaptation, he found that he slept more profoundly than he had ever done before and woke "full of energy and limpid freshness."

Without the pressures of a hectic social and professional life, Leigh Fermor found that he enjoyed an entirely new vitality and peace. Even major worries "slid away into some distant limbo." The regimen which had initially seemed so constricting gave him a sense of "absolute, godless freedom"; work became easier, and the abbey became the "reverse of a tomb...a castle hanging in mid-air beyond the reach of ordinary troubles and vexations." As Leigh Fermor listened to the monks chanting the psalms and prayers of the Divine Office, he had intimations of transcendence and enlightenment. When he eventually left the abbey and returned to Paris, the secular world at first appeared "an inferno of noise and vulgarity"; it was as difficult to resume his ordinary life as it had been to adapt to the monastic silence and isolation.

Even a limited experience of the monastic life can introduce people to the real meaning of religion far more effectively than abstract theological beliefs. In the eleventh century, the Benedictine monks of Cluny, near Paris, made a massive effort to educate the laity of Europe, who were woefully ignorant of Christianity. They did not attempt to teach laypeople the complicated doctrines of the Church. Instead they sent them on pilgrimage, which, under the aegis of Cluny, became a hugely popular activity. While they traveled to their holy destination—to Rome, Compostella, or a local shrine—laymen and laywomen had to live for a time like monks. The pilgrims turned their backs on their normal lives and lived a communal life; they prayed together; the hardships of the journey were a form of asceticism; they were celibate for the duration of the pilgrimage and were forbidden to fight or bear arms. The experience was designed to transform their behavior in such a way that they would intuit the deeper meaning of Christian faith.

I myself experienced something similar. I did not find enlightenment in my convent because I was not suited to the religious order I had chosen. For years after ceasing to be a nun, I wanted nothing to do with religion. It was only when, after a series of career disasters, I found myself living alone and in silence while researching my book *A History of God* that the religious texts I was studying began to make sense. Theology is a form of poetry, an attempt to express the inexpressible, and you cannot read a sonnet by Shakespeare in the chatter and tumult of a party. These truths are elusive and resist easy conceptualization. You have to open yourself to a sacred text with a quiet receptive mind. Gradually I found that without the distraction of constant conversation, the words on the page began to speak directly to my inner self.

I sympathize with Leigh Fermor, when he remarked one day to the Abbot what a blessed relief it was to refrain from talking all day long. "Yes," the Abbot replied; "in the outside world, speech is gravely abused." Our world is even more noisy than it was in the 1950s, when Leigh Fermor wrote this book: piped music and mobile phones jangle ceaselessly, and silence and solitude are shunned as alien and unnatural. We expect instant communication and seek knowledge at the click of a mouse. We are also living at a time of competing certainties and religious stridency. It is important to realize that there are more profound and authentic ways of being religious. Very few of us can be contemplative nuns or monks, but we can learn to appreciate their way of experiencing the sacred and integrate something of this gentle, silent discipline into our own lives. This gem of a book can help us to do just that.

—KAREN ARMSTRONG

AUTHOR'S INTRODUCTION

As THE reader may gather from occasional hints in the
following pages, I was hindered by several disabilities
from sharing to the utmost all the advantages a stranger
may gain from monastic sojourns. Hints they must remain as they touch on perplexities that have little bearing
on the main drift of this book; but it is worth mentioning
them in order to make it clear that there are serious limitations to my authority in writing of these matters, and to
prepare the reader for the shortcomings attendant on in-
complete knowledge and experience.

But, in spite of these private limitations I was profoundly affected by the places I have described. I am not
sure what these feelings amount to, but they are deeper
than mere interest and curiosity, and more important
than the pleasure an historian or an æsthete finds in ancient buildings and liturgy; for I could have seen the former in many places and the latter—though seldom,
perhaps, as well performed as at St. Wandrille or Solesmes
—I had always known.

The kindness of the monks has something to do with
this. But more important was the discovery of a capacity

for solitude and (on however humble a level compared to that of most people who resort to monasteries) for the recollectedness and clarity of spirit that accompany the silent monastic life. For, in the seclusion of a cell—an existence whose quietness is only varied by the silent meals, the solemnity of ritual and long solitary walks in the woods—the troubled waters of the mind grow still and clear, and much that is hidden away and all that clouds it floats to the surface and can be skimmed away; and after a time one reaches a state of peace that is unthought of in the ordinary world. This is so different from any normal experience, that it makes the stranger suspect that he has been the beneficiary (in spite, or in the teeth, of recalcitrance or scepticism or plain incapacity for belief) of a supernatural windfall or an unconsciously appropriated share in the spiritual activity that is always at work in monasteries. Even someone like myself—no stranger to the disabilities I have just mentioned—when thrown by chance in touch with monasticism, can glean from it much of the healing and mysterious enchantment for which, among other purposes, monasteries were built.

It is impossible for anyone who has had even this slight experience not to feel, at the sight of empty monasteries, a sorrow sharper than the regret of an antiquarian. Something of this elegiac sadness overhangs the rock-monasteries of Cappadocia that I have tried to describe. But, for us in the West, because of all such relics they are the most compelling mementoes of the life that once animated them, the ruined abbeys of England that have remained desolate since the Reformation will always be the most moving and tragic. For there is no riddle here. We know the function and purpose of every fragment and the exact details of the holy life that should be sheltering there. We know, too, the miserable and wanton story of their destruction and their dereliction, and have only to close our eyes for a second for the imagination to rebuild the towers and the pinnacles and summon to our ears the quiet rumour of monkish activity and the sound of bells melted long ago. They emerge in the fields like the peaks of a vanished Atlantis drowned four centuries deep. The gutted cloisters stand uselessly among the furrows and only broken pillars mark the former symmetry of the aisles and ambulatories. Surrounded by elder-flower, with their bases entangled in bracken and blackberry and bridged at their summits with arches and broken spandrels that fly spinning over the tree-tops in slender trajectories, the clustering pillars suspend the great empty circumference of a rose-window in the rook-haunted sky. It is as though some tremendous Gregorian chant had been interrupted hundreds of years ago to hang there petrified at its climax ever since.

—P. L. F.

1957

It is hard to believe that these monastic travels and halts took place thirty years ago. Asked point blank, I would have said: ten at the outside, for they remain clearer in detail than some later tracts of life that have been blurred or swept away.

I have seen a number of monasteries in the interim: La Pierre qui Vire, St. Benoît-sur-Loire, Fossanova, Trisulti, Monte Olivetto, Subiaco, the ruins of Monte Cassino, the Charterhouses of Pavia and Jerez, Guadalupe and Yuste, Beuron, Gottweig and Melk, The Merced of Cuzco, Santa Catalina at Arequipa in Peru, the familiar monasteries of Greece and those very early Arabic- and Aramaic-speaking foundations among the canyons near Damascus. But these were a part of wider travels. The only ones where, at wide intervals, I have made sojourns like the ones I have tried to describe have been at St. Wandrille and Quarr Abbey. Each time they seem surer abodes of faith, wisdom, learning, goodness and dignified and scrupulous observance, and much survives in places like these which otherwise have vanished or changed. Listening to the singing of the Hours in the language of fifth- or sixth-century Western Christendom, one can forget the alterations of the twentieth and feel that the lifeline of notes and syllables between the Early Church and today is still intact: that these, indeed, might have been the sung words to which King Aethelbert and Queen Bertha listened when St. Augustine first set foot in the Isle of Thanet.

When it first came out, the book struck lucky with reviewers and with readers outside monasteries, and—insofar as I could tell, which is not much—inside as well. But one monastic critic brought it rather sternly to task: I had picked up a superficial acquaintance with monastic matters while staying as a guest; to write about them was intrusive and indiscreet. It was an aspect which had not struck me as it ought to have done, but I saw at once and all too clearly what he meant. I was very downcast and I wrote to the same periodical with a rather clumsy apology; and this, soon afterwards, evoked a letter from a monk whom I had not met. Without contradicting any of the strictures, he inferred, with great tact and kindness, that his colleague had been severe in this instance and that the innocent intention was clear.

The book was based—whole passages of it word for word—on letters I wrote at the time to a correspondent (whom I later married) without the remotest thought of publication. I was living a lot in France, much under the influence of Huysmans, and I haunted quays and bookshops and libraries. Starting with Montalembert's *Les Moines d'Occident*, I read everything about monasticism and, above all, French monastic history that I could find. It was then that I thought of putting these months together in literary form; and when at last the text was in proof, I returned to St. Wandrille to show it to the Abbot. As the reader will see, I liked and admired him greatly; he was a scholarly, civilized and good man; I was anxious about his opinion; and the overall impression was encouraging. He liked the descriptive and historical parts about his Abbey to which he was deeply attached and there were mistakes that could be remedied. I said I must have gone off the rails sometimes. "From the monk's point of view," he said with a smile, "of course you have! But these are the parts to me that make it interesting." I took these words as I hoped they were meant. As long as I made my own position clear, he said, he could see nothing against it.

The Abbot's remarks were unofficial and private; we were on friendly terms; he may have been letting me down lightly; and my later correspondent had obviously sought to cheer me up, which indeed he had done; whereas the monastic critic was writing from an official standpoint, especially from that of an older generation of monks; and, of course, he was right. It had not occurred to me how jarring, to such a reader, these lucubrations of an outsider might be—even opinions like those on the survival of Latin plain-song two paragraphs back, let alone any tentative steps into deeper water. There is only one demand of monastery guests, especially those in my category: they should not in any way disturb the life of the monastery. As time advances, the stress of work and the threat of outside distraction make the need for silence and privacy more urgent than ever and publicity of any kind proportionately more to be dreaded. I would have written differently now, or perhaps not written at all. This is where I had gone astray and that is why the apology still stands.

All this being so, I wondered what to do when after so

many years the question of another edition cropped up. Perhaps the passage of three decades had been on my side, for I was sustained by the discovery that opinions in the quarter I cared about—inasmuch as any such opinions existed, or that I could judge of them—were favourable. Their drift was this: however wide of the mark some of it might be, there were redeeming points enough for a reprint not to come amiss. It would also be a chance to insert the thoughts contained in the last paragraph. I considered revising and cutting the text; but there is not much of it and long-published matter when tampered with may crumble to bits; so here, surrounded by a most necessary cloud of caveats and provisos, it unregenerately is; and I cannot suppress a feeling of relief that a chapter of life that was so important to me has been given a reprieve.

—P. L. F.

1982

A TIME TO KEEP SILENCE

Questi altri fochi tutti contemplanti
   uomini furo, accesi di quel caldo
che fa nascere i fiori e i frutti santi.

Qui è Maccario, qui è Romoaldo,
   qui son li frati miei, che dentro ai chiostri
fermar li piedi e tennero il cor saldo.

DANTE: Paradiso XXII, 46–51

To every thing there is a season and a
time to every purpose under heaven…
…a time to keep silence and a time to speak.

Ecclesiastes: III, 1 & 7

To my mother

THE ABBEY OF
ST. WANDRILLE DE FONTANELLE

WITH CURIOSITY and misgiving I walked up hill from the Rouen-Yvetot road towards the Abbey of St. Wandrille. I had spent an abominable night in Rouen in a small hotel near the station where a procession of nightmares had been punctuated by the noise of trains arriving and leaving with a crashing and whistling and an escape of steam and smoke which, after a week's noctambulism in Paris, turned my night into a period of acute and apparently interminable agony. Even the misty windings of the lower Seine, the fat green fields and Indian files of poplars, among which the bus had travelled next morning, could not dispel my mood of sluggishness and depression; and now, climbing the hot road through the late summer woods, I wondered if my project had not better be abandoned. What I dreaded almost more than success was an immediate failure. If there was no room at the Abbey, or if for some other reason the monks could not receive me, I should have to return to Paris and readjust my plans for the next few weeks. I was arriving unknown and unannounced, a citizen of the heretic island across the Channel, without even the excuse that I wished to go into retreat; I was, in fact, in search of somewhere quiet and cheap to stay while I continued to work on a book that I was writing. A friend in Paris had told me that St. Wandrille was one of the oldest and most beautiful Benedictine Abbeys in France; and I had made my plans and set out...

It was Sunday, and the gatehouse was full of visitors who, just emerged from Mass, were buying pictures, medals, rosaries and assorted *bondieuserie*. A harassed monk in horn-rimmed glasses was answering innumerable questions; and a quarter of an hour had gone by before I managed, with considerable trepidation, to explain my proposal. He listened sympathetically, and asked me to return after he had spoken to the Abbot. When at last his black-robed figure reappeared across the garden, I saw that he was smiling. Seizing my heavy bag, "The most reverend Father Abbot can receive you," he announced, "and wishes you welcome."

A few moments later a door had shut out the noise of the Sunday visitors and a silent maze of white staircases and passages swallowed us up. The monk opened a door and said, "Here is your cell." It was a high seventeenth-century room with a comfortable bed, a *prie-dieu*, a writing-table, a tapestry chair, a green adjustable reading-lamp, and a rather disturbing crucifix on the whitewashed stone walls. The window looked out over a grassy court-yard, in which a small fountain played, over the grey flank of the monastery buildings and the wall that screened the

Abbey from the half-timbered houses of the village. A vista of forest flowed away beyond. In the middle of the writing-table stood a large inkwell, a tray full of pens and a pad into which new blotting paper had just been fitted. I had only time to unpack my clothes and papers and books before a great bell began ringing and the monk, who was the guest-master, returned to lead me to the refectory for the midday meal. As we walked, the buildings changed in period from the architecture of the eighteenth and seventeenth centuries to Gothic; and we halted at length by the piscina in an ogival cloister of the utmost beauty, outside a great carved door where several other visitors had also been assembled. The guest-master shepherded us into the refectory in which the Abbot, a tall, white-haired, patrician figure with a black skull-cap and a gold pectoral cross on a green cord, was waiting to receive us. To each of the guests he spoke a few words; and some, sinking upon one knee, kissed the great emerald on his right hand. To me he addressed a polite formula in English that had obviously been acquired at some remote period from a governess. A novice advanced with a silver ewer and a basin; the Abbot poured a little water over our hands, a towel was offered, and our welcome, according to Benedictine custom, was complete.

The singing of grace continued for several minutes; and, when we sat down, I found myself between two visiting priests, their birettas folded flat beside their plates on the long guest-table in the middle of the refectory, just below the Abbot's dais. Down the walls of this immense hall the tables of the monks were ranged in two unbroken lines, and behind them a row of Romanesque pilasters with interlocking Norman arches formed a shallow arcade. The place had an aura of immense antiquity. Grey stone walls soared to a Gothic timber roof, and, above the Abbot's table, a giant crucifix was suspended. As the monks tucked their napkins into their collars with a simultaneous and uniform gesture, an unearthly voice began to speak in Latin from the shadows overhead and, peering towards it, I caught sight, at the far end of the refectory, of a pillared bay twenty feet up which projected like a martin's nest, accessible only by some hidden stairway. This hanging pulpit framed the head and shoulders of a monk, reading from a desk by the light of a lamp which hollowed a glowing alcove out of the penumbra. Loudspeakers relayed his sing-song voice. Meanwhile, the guest-master and a host of aproned monks waited at the tables, putting tureens of vegetable soup before us and dropping into our plates two boiled eggs, which were followed by a dish of potatoes and lentils, then by an endive salad, and finally by discs of camembert, to be eaten with excellent bread from the Abbey bakery. Every now and then a monk left his place, and knelt for a few minutes before the Abbot's table. At a sign from the Abbot, he would rise, make a deep bow, and withdraw.... Inspired probably by Victorian oleographs of monastic life, I had expected a prodigious flow of red wine. The metal jugs on our tables contained, alas, only water.

The recitation had now changed from Latin to French, delivered in the same sepulchral, and, to me, largely unintelligible, monotone. A few proper names emerged—Louis Phillipe, Dupanloup, Lacordaire, Guizot, Thiers, Gambetta, Montalembert—and it was clear that we were listening to a chapter of French nineteenth-century history. This stilted manner of treating a lay text sounded absurd at first and oddly sanctimonious; its original object, I discovered, had been both to act as a curb on histrionic vanity and to minimise the difficulties of the unlearned reader in the days of St. Benedict. Throughout the entire meal no other word was spoken. The tables were cleared, and the monks, their eyes downcast, sat with their hands crossed beneath their scapulars. The Abbot thereupon gave a sharp tap with a little mallet; the reader, abandoning his text, bowed so low over the balustrade that it seemed that he would fall out and then intoned the words *Tu autem Domine misercre nobis*; all rose, and bowing to a rectangular position with their hands crossed on their knees, chanted a long thanksgiving. Straightening, they turned and bowed to the Abbot and, still chanting, moved slowly out of the refectory in double file around two sides of the cloisters, into the church and up the central aisle. Here each pair of monks genuflected, inclined their heads one to another, and made their way to opposite stalls. The chanting continued for about eight minutes, then the entry was gravely reversed. As they reached the cloisters, the files of black figures broke up and dispersed throughout the Abbey.

Back in my cell, I sat down before the new blotter and pens and sheets of clean foolscap. I had asked for quiet and solitude and peace, and here it was; all I had to do now was to write. But an hour passed, and nothing happened. It began to rain over the woods outside, and a mood of depression and of unspeakable loneliness suddenly felled me like a hammer-stroke. On the inner side of my door, the printed "Rules for the Guests' Wing" contained a mass of cheerless information. The monks' day, I learned, began at 4 a.m., with the offices of Matins and Lauds, followed by periods for private masses and reading and meditation. A guest's day began at 8:15 with the office of Prime and breakfast in silence. At 10 the Conventual High Mass was sandwiched between Tierce and Sext. Luncheon at 1. Nones and Vespers at 5 p.m. Supper at 7:30, then, at 8:30, Compline and to bed in silence at 9. All meals, the rules pointed out, were eaten in silence: one was enjoined to take one's "recreation" apart, and only to speak to the monks with the Abbot's permission; not to make a noise walking about the Abbey; not to smoke in the cloisters; to talk in a low voice, and rigorously to observe the periods of silence. They struck me as impossibly forbidding. So much silence and sobriety! The place assumed the character of an enormous tomb, a necropolis of which I was the only living inhabitant.

The first bell was already ringing for Vespers, and I went down to the cloisters and watched the monks assemble in silence for their processional entrance. They had put on, over their habits and scapulars, black cowls: flowing gowns with hoods into which those of their ordinary habits fitted, and so voluminous that the wearers appeared to glide rather than walk. Their hands were invisibly joined, like those of mandarins, in the folds of their sleeves, and the stooped faces, deep in the tunnel of their pointed hoods, were almost completely hidden. A wonderful garb for anonymity! They were exact echoes of Mrs. Radcliffe's villainous monastics and of the miscreants of Protestant anti-popish literature. Yet they looked not so much sinister as desperately sad. Only in the refectory and the church was I able to see their faces; and, as I sat at Vespers watching them, now cowled, now uncovered, according to the progress of the liturgy, they appeared preternaturally pale, some of them nearly green. The bone-structure of their faces lay nearly always close beneath the surface. But, though a deep hollow often accentuated the shadow under the cheekbone, their faces were virtually without a wrinkle, and it was this creaseless haggardness that made their faces so distinct from any others. How different, I thought, from the fierce, whiskered, brigand-faces of the Greek monks of Athos or the Meteora, whose eyes smoulder and flash and twinkle under brows that are always tied up in knots of rage or laughter or concentration or suddenly relaxed into bland, Olympian benevolence. The gulf between the cenobites of Rome and those of Byzantium was often in my mind. A cowled figure would flit past in silence, and all at once, with a smile, I would remember Fathers Dionysios and Gabriel, Brothers Theophylaktos, Christ and Polycarp, my bearded, long-haired, cylinder-hatted, war-time hosts and protectors in Crete, pouring out raki, cracking walnuts, singing mountain songs, stripping and assembling pistols, cross-questioning me interminably about Churchill, and snoring under olive trees while the sun's beams fell perpendicularly on the Libyan Sea. . . . But here, in the Abbey's boreal shadows, there was never a smile or a frown. No seismic shock of hilarity or anger or fear could ever, I felt, have disturbed the tranquil geography of those monastic features. Their eyelids were always downcast; and, if now and then they were raised, no treacherous glint appeared, nothing but a sedulously cultivated calmness, withdrawal and mansuetude and occasionally an expression of remote and burnt-out melancholy. The muted light in the church suspended a filament between us, reproducing the exact atmosphere of an early seventeenth-century Spanish studio in which—tonsured, waxen, austere and exsanguinous—were bowed in prayer the models of Zurbarán and El Greco. Not for nothing had these painters followed so closely after St. Theresa and St. John of the Cross, and so faithfully portrayed the external stigmata of monastic obedience, prayer, meditation, mortification and mystical experiment—the traces left by the soul's dark night, by the scaling of heavenly mountains and the exploration of interior mansions. As the monks dispersed after Vespers and, a few hours later, after Compline, I had a sensation of the temperature of life falling to zero, the blood running every second thinner and slower as if the heart might in the end imperceptibly stop beating. These men really lived as if each day were their last, at peace with the world, shriven, fortified by the sacraments, ready at any moment to cease upon the midnight with no pain. Death, when it came, would be the easiest of change-overs. The silence, the appearance, the complexion and the gait of ghosts they had already; the final step would be only a matter of detail. "And then," I continued to myself, "when the golden gates swing open with an angelic fanfare, what happens then? Won't these quiet people feel lost among streets paved with beryl and sardonyx and jacinth? After so many years of retirement, they would surely prefer eternal twilight and a cypress or two...." The Abbey was now fast asleep but it seemed ridiculously early—about the moment when friends in Paris (whom I suddenly and acutely missed) were still uncertain where to dine. Having finished a flask of Calvados, which I had bought in Rouen, I sat at my desk in a condition of overwhelming gloom and *accidie*. As I looked round the white box of my cell, I suffered what Pascal declared to be the cause of all human evils.

———

The history of the Abbey of St. Wandrille typifies French religious and secular life through nearly three-quarters of the Christian era. Early chronicles still in existence, and the famous *Gesta Abbatum*, tell of its beginnings when the north of France was divided up into the shadowy realms of Neustria and Austrasia, regions of forest and swamp which only the wolves and wild boar inhabited. The full name of the monastery is L'Abbaye de St. Wandrille de Fontanelle, linking together its saintly founder and the little river—*ruissel et fontaine de merveilleuse beauté*—on whose banks, in A.D. 649, Wandrille, with a handful of monks, cleared the forest and built the first conventual buildings. Wandrille came of a family of some standing. He was a cousin of Pepin the Old and of the Mayor of the Austrasian palace and himself began life as a courtier of King Dagobert. But he abandoned the court and the prospects of a splendid marriage and wandered south from monastery to monastery, remaining a number of years in the cloisters of St. Columbanus, the stern Irish Abbot of Bobbio in Cisalpine Gaul. Bobbio he only abandoned to found the Abbey that bears his name. Here, after performing countless miracles and casting out numbers of devils, he died in an odour of sanctity. The Abbey grew and prospered and no fewer than seventeen of his successors were canonised. During the abbacy of St. Hugh, nephew of the Charles Martel who drove the

Moors from south-west France about half a century before the reign of Charlemagne, the Abbey reached its territorial apogee; for St. Hugh, besides being abbot of the great foundation of Jumièges, was archbishop of Rouen and bishop of Paris and Bayeux, and the Abbey possessed parishes and priories all over the north of France and as far afield as Burgundy and even Provence. From that time, the fortunes of the Abbey varied in the hands of succeeding abbots. Sometimes this dignitary was more of a warrior than a cleric, a figure in chain-armour adept at archery and swordsmanship rather than at his pastoral office; and sometimes a great ecclesiastic, inspired by whose unction and zeal the Abbey became a centre of scholarship: founding schools, enlarging the library, and illuminating and transcribing manuscripts. In the ninth century the wing- and horn-helmeted Normans arrived in narrow ships from Scandinavia and conquered and laid waste the whole of the region. The Abbey was soon a ruin, and the monks wandered for a century with no possessions except the relics of their founders. But they were back by the middle of the tenth century, building the cloisters and church and sending out monks to reform the relaxed community of Mont Saint-Michel. The Abbey lay in the heart of Duke William's recruiting ground for the invasion of England; and, after the conquest, St. Wandrille was endowed with four livings in England. (Incidentally, no specific Act ever having been passed to abolish the privilege, the present Abbot is still a canon of Salisbury

Cathedral.)* A terrible fire ravaged the Abbey in the thirteenth century; but from that time, building and expansion continued; spires and pinnacles soared into the sky; and, in 1395, Boniface IX bestowed on the Abbot and his successors the privilege of the mitre and crosier. The Abbey was in the centre of the dynastic troubles of the Plantagenets and the Valois; and during the Hundred Years War it was, to the detriment of religious discipline, less a convent than a citadel.

In 1502 the blight of Commendation, an evil whose effects on monastic life of France were as drastic as the phylloxera that centuries later ravaged her vineyards, fell upon St. Wandrille. By this system commendatory abbots—courtiers who were never monks and often not even in holy orders—received abbeys and priories as rewards for service to the State or as the fruits of intrigue or nepotism, swallowing two-thirds of the monastic revenues, and seldom approaching their conventual fiefs nearer than Versailles. St. Wandrille became the chattel of a series of absent grandees; yet somehow the monks succeeded in keeping their life and discipline intact. St. Wandrille seems to have been spared by none of the disas-

---

*By the twelfth century St. Wandrille's English possessions (most of which, however, were dispersed long before the Dissolution) were fairly large. The Abbey possessed, among others, the parishes of Whitchurch, Bridport and Burton in Dorset; Upavon, Manningford and Sherston in Wiltshire; Wandesford in the see of Winchester, Ecclesfield in Yorkshire and Towcester in Northamptonshire, and a further impressive group of advowsons, tithes, glebes, hides, mills, woods and other rural properties.

ters of French history. She played her part in the Fronde and the Religious Wars, and in 1562 was desecrated and pillaged by the Huguenots of Montgomery. In 1631, three hundred years almost to a day after its erection, the Gothic belfry collapsed, and, at about the same time, the reforms of the Maurists were imported to the Abbey: a measure that bolstered up the morale of the monks through the period of philosophic doubt that followed. The Abbey had fallen a victim to every material calamity, but, from the dangers of Port Royal, Jansenism, Quietism and Gallicanism, its orthodoxy emerged unscathed.

With the French Revolution came the abolition of all the religious houses of France. The monks were scattered, the library was split up and auctioned and the conventual buildings were sold. Most of the old abbey church was pulled down, and the masonry carted off and disposed of by the ton as building material. In 1863 the property was bought and reconstituted—romantically and often most unsuitably—by an Irishman called the Marquis, and later the Duke, de Stacpoole, who belonged to a family of Irish landowners with a curious knack for acquiring foreign titles, his father having been created a viscount and count by Louis XVIII, and marquis and duke by Popes Leo XII and Gregory XVI. This curious nobleman eventually took holy orders and became a Monsignor and a domestic chaplain to the Pope; and the oldest villagers still just remember the Union Jack flying from the Abbey walls during the German occupation that followed the Franco-Prussian war.

By 1894, after nearly a century's absence, the Benedictines had returned to their old home under the abbacy of the famous Dom Joseph Pothier, one of the great pioneers in the restoration of Gregorian plain-song. But in 1901, the anti-monastic legislation of the Waldeck-Rousseau Government, launched by the politician derisively known as *le Petit Père Combe*, again emptied the abbeys of France. The monks of St. Wandrille found refuge in Belgium, and the Abbey was once more in the hands of strangers. Its last secular inhabitants were Maurice Maeterlinck and Georgette Leblanc, and during their tenancy it became the background for elaborate semi-amateur theatricals. *Macbeth* and *Pelléas et Melisande* were performed by torchlight in the cloisters and refectory, and Maeterlinck, in pursuit of inspiration, smoking furiously and followed by a cascade of barking terriers, would career all morning long round the cloisters on roller-skates.... By 1930, however, the monks were reinstated. Many—for the French constitution admits no exemption for the occupants of religious houses—were called up at the outbreak of war to serve as officers, non-commissioned officers and men. The remainder continued to keep the Abbey going throughout the occupation. During the liberation of Normandy, St. Wandrille was in the thick of the battle area, and part of the seventeenth-century buildings were destroyed by Allied bombs. Sixty or seventy choir-monks and lay-brothers—representatives, after exactly thirteen centuries, of a monastic brotherhood that nothing seems to be able to destroy—now inhabit, as if nothing had ever ruffled the quiet rhythm of their history, the ancient buildings; and at their head reigns the Abbot who had bade me welcome in the refectory, le Révérendissime Père Abbé, Dom Gabriel Gontard, seventy-eighth successor of St. Wandrille.

———

My first feelings in the monastery changed: I lost the sensation of circumambient and impending death, of being by mistake locked up in a catacomb. I think the alteration must have taken about four days. The mood of dereliction persisted some time, a feeling of loneliness and flatness that always accompanies the transition from urban excess to a life of rustic solitude. Here in the Abbey, in absolutely unfamiliar surroundings, this miserable bridge-passage was immensely widened. One is prone to accept the idea of monastic life as a phenomenon that has always existed, and to dismiss it from the mind without further analysis or comment; only by living for a while in a monastery can one quite grasp its staggering difference from the ordinary life that we lead. The two ways of life do not share a single attribute; and the thoughts, ambitions, sounds, light, time and mood that surround the inhabitants of a cloister are not only unlike anything to which one is accustomed, but in some curious way, seem its exact reverse. The period during which normal standards recede and the strange new world becomes reality is slow, and, at first, acutely painful.

To begin with, I slept badly at night and fell asleep during the day, felt restless alone in my cell and depressed by the lack of alcohol, the disappearance of which had caused a sudden halt in the customary monsoon. The most remarkable preliminary symptoms were the variations of my need of sleep. After initial spells of insomnia, nightmare and falling asleep by day, I found that my capacity for sleep was becoming more and more remarkable: till the hours I spent in or on my bed vastly outnumbered the hours I spent awake; and my sleep was so profound that I might have been under the influence of some hypnotic drug. For two days, meals and the offices in the church—Mass, Vespers and Compline—were almost my only lucid moments. Then began an extraordinary transformation: this extreme lassitude dwindled to nothing; night shrank to five hours of light, dreamless and perfect sleep, followed by awakenings full of energy and limpid freshness. The explanation is simple enough: the desire for talk, movement and nervous expression that I had transported from Paris found, in this silent place, no response or foil, evoked no single echo; after miserably gesticulating for a while in a vacuum, it languished and finally died for lack of any stimulus or nourishment. Then the tremendous accumulation of tiredness, which must be the common property of all our contemporaries, broke loose and swamped everything. No demands, once I had emerged from that flood of sleep, were made upon my nervous energy: there were no automatic drains, such as conversation at meals, small talk, catching trains, or the hundred anxious trivialities that poison everyday life. Even the major causes of guilt and anxiety had slid away into some distant limbo and not only failed to emerge in the small hours as tormentors but appeared to have lost their dragonish validity. This new dispensation left nineteen hours a day of absolute and god-like freedom. Work became easier every moment; and, when I was not working, I was either exploring the Abbey and the neighbouring countryside, or reading. The Abbey became the reverse of a tomb—not, indeed, a Thelema or Nepenthe, but a silent university, a country house, a castle hanging in mid-air beyond the reach of ordinary troubles and vexations. A verse from the office of Compline expresses the same thought; and it was no doubt an unconscious memory of it that prompted me to put it down: *Altissimum posuisti refugium tuum... non accedet ad te malum et flagellum non appropinquabit tabernaculo tuo.*

Slowly, the monks changed from two-dimensional figures on counter-reformation canvasses and became real people, though the guest-master remained almost my only interlocutor. This sympathetic figure, Father Tierce, lived in the guest-house, and was at first my sole line with the monastic life around me. In the rule of St. Benedict, the offices of guest-master and cellarer are, after the rank of abbot and prior, those that call for the solidest faith and character, since they bring the holder into daily and hourly contact with the influences and distractions of the outside world. My particular friend was a compendium of charity and unselfishness, whose one study appeared to be the happiness and comfort of his charges; finding places for them during the services, seeing that their cells were comfortable, warning them of mealtimes, and generally steering them through all the reefs and shallows of the monastic routine; beaming through horn-rimmed spectacles, then always bustling away with a swirl of robes on some benevolent errand. It was he who put me in the hands of the librarian, a young and elaborately educated choir-monk who made me free of a vast book-lined labyrinth occupying the whole of a seventeenth-century wing. The library was beautifully kept, and, considering the Abbey's vicissitudes, enormous. Vellum-bound folios and quartos receded in vistas, and thousands of ancient and modern works on theology, canon law, dogma, patrology, patristics, hagiography, mysticism and even magic, and almost as many on secular history, art and travel. Poetry, drama, heraldry, the whole of Greek and Roman literature, a special library on the history and geography of Normandy, an extremely rich and up-to-date reference library, Hebrew, Arabic, Cyriac and Chaldean and hundreds of English books, completed the catalogue. The father librarian gave me a key and his permission to take as many books as I liked to my cell. Like all monastic libraries it possessed a number of volumes that had been placed on the index because they offended against theological orthodoxy; and a number, considered damaging to the peace of monastic life, were locked up in a depository known as the *Enfer*. On various occasions, following up trains of enquiry, I asked for books from both sources, and obtained them without difficulty. Several monks were usually working in the library, reading and writing at the desks, or climbing the ladders in pursuit of recondite knowledge.*

As, gradually, I found myself talking to them, I was surprised by the conversation of the monks with whom I came in contact. I found no trace of the Dark Ages here, no hint of necropolitan gloom or bigotry, still less of the ghastly breeziness that is such an embarrassing characteristic of many English clerics. There was no doubt of the respect in which they held the cause to which their lives were devoted; but their company was like that of any civilised well-educated Frenchman, with all the balance, erudition and wit that one expected, the only difference being a gentleness, a lack of haste, and a calmness which is common to the whole community. Seeing them at their devotions and in silence at meals, I had imagined them to

---

*Of the beautiful St. Wandrille Breviary printed in 1535, only one copy survives, now in the Bodleian Library. It is not known how the Breviary, printed only a year before the Dissolution, found its way to England, as all links between the Abbey and its former priories and parishes in England had long been broken, and the Breviary was printed with the purpose of perpetuating, for the monks of St. Wandrille, certain minor liturgical differences peculiar to the Abbey. It is a treasure that the Abbey sighs to possess.

be almost incapable of laughter, of curiosity or any of the more ordinary manifestations of personal feeling.

After the first postulate of belief, without which the life of a monk would be farcical and intolerable, the dominating factor of monastic existence is a belief in the necessity and efficacy of prayer; and it is only by attempting to grasp the importance of this principle—a principle so utterly remote from every tendency of modern secular thought—to the monks who practise it, that one can hope to understand the basis of monasticism. This is especially true of the contemplative orders, like the Benedictines, Carthusians, Carmelites, Cistercians, Camaldulese and Sylvestrines; for the others—like the Franciscans, Dominicans or the Jesuits—are brotherhoods organised for action. They travel, teach, preach, convert, organise, plan, heal and nurse; and the material results they achieve make them, if not automatically admirable, at least comprehensible to the Time-Spirit. They get results; they deliver the goods. But what (the Time-Spirit asks) what good do the rest do, immured in monasteries far from all contact with the world? The answer is—if the truth of the Christian religion and the efficacy of prayer are both dismissed as baseless—no more than any other human beings who lead a good life, make (for they support themselves) no economic demands on the community, harm no one and respect their neighbours. But, should the two principles be admitted—particularly, for the purposes of this particular theme, the latter—their power for good is incalculable. Belief in this power, and in the necessity of worshipping God daily and hourly, is the mainspring of Benedictine life. It was this belief that, in the sixth century, drove St. Benedict into the solitude of a cave in the Sabine gorges and, after three years of private ascesis, prompted him to found the first Benedictine communities. His book, *The Rule of St. Benedict*—seventy-three short and sagacious chapters explaining the theory and codifying the practice of the cenobitic life—is aimed simply at securing for his monks protection against the world, so that nothing should interfere with the utmost exploitation of this enormous force. The vows embracing poverty, chastity and obedience were destined to smite from these men all fetters that chained them to the world, to free them for action, for the worship of God and the practice of prayer; for the pursuit, in short, of sanctity. Worship found its main expression, of course, in the Mass; but the offices of the seven canonical hours that follow the Night Office of Matins—Lauds, Prime, Tierce, Sext, Nones, Vespers and Compline, a cycle that begins in the small hours of the night and finishes after sunset—kept, and keep the monks on parade, as it were, with an almost military rigour. Their programme for the day involves three-and-a-half or four hours in church. But other periods, quite separate from the time devoted to study, are set aside for the reading of the martyrology in the chapter-house, for self-examination, private prayer and meditation. One has only to glance at the mass of devotional and mystical works which have appeared throughout the Christian era to get an idea of the difficulty, the complexity, the pitfalls and the rewards of this form of spiritual exercise. However strange these values may appear to the *homme moyen sensuel*, such are the pursuits that absorb much of a monk's life. They range from a repetition of the simpler prayers, sometimes tallied by the movement of beads through the fingers, to an advanced intellectual skill in devotion and meditation; and occasionally rise to those hazardous mystical journeys of the soul which culminate, at the end of the purgative and illuminative periods, in blinding moments of union with the Godhead; experiences which the poverty of language compels the mystics who experience them to describe in the terminology of profane love: a kind of personal, face-to-face intimacy, the very inkling of which, since Donne, Quarles, Herbert, Vaughan and Traherne wrote their poems, has drained away from life in England. With this daily, unflagging stream of worship, a volume of prayer ascends, of which, if it is efficacious, we are all the beneficiaries. Between people pledged to those spiritual allegiances, "*Pray for me*" and "*Give me your blessing*" are no polite formulæ, but requests for definite, effective acts. And it is easy to imagine the value and fame, before the growth of scepticism, of men whose lives were spent hammering out in silent factories these imponderable but priceless benefits. They are the anonymous well-wishers who reduce the moral overdraft of mankind, *les paratonnerres* (as Huysmans says) *de la société.* Life, for a monk, is shorter than the flutter of an eyelid in comparison to eternity, and this fragment of time flits past in the worship of God, the salvation of his soul, and in humble intercession for the souls of his fellow exiles from felicity.

Their values have remained stable while those of the world have passed through kaleidoscopic changes. It is curious to hear, from the outside world in the throes of its yearly metamorphoses, cries of derision levelled at the monastic life. How shallow, whatever views may be held concerning the fundamental truth or fallacy of the Christian religion, are these accusations of hypocrisy, sloth, selfishness and escapism! The life of monks passes in a state of white-hot conviction and striving to which there is never a holiday; and no living man, after all, is in a position to declare their premises true or false. They have foresworn the pleasures and rewards of a world whose values they consider meaningless; and they alone have as a body confronted the terrifying problem of eternity, abandoning everything to help their fellow-men and themselves to meet it.

Worship, then, and prayer are the *raison d'être* of the Benedictine order; and anything else, even their great achievements as scholars and architects and doctors of the church, is subsidiary. They were, however, for centuries the only guardians of literature, the classics, scholarship and the humanities in a world of which the confusion can best be compared to our own atomic era. For a long period, after the great epoch of Benedictine scholarship at Cluny, the Maurist Benedictine Abbey of St. Germain-des-Prés was the most important residuary of learning and science in Europe. Only a few ivy-clad ruins remain, just visible between *zazou* suits and existentialist haircuts from the terrace of the *Deux Magots*. But in scores of abbeys all over Europe, the same liberal traditions survive and prosper. Other by-products of their life were the beautiful buildings in which I was living, and the unparalleled calm that prevailed there. At St. Wandrille I was inhabiting at last a tower of solid ivory, and I, not the monks, was the escapist. For my hosts, the Abbey was a springboard into eternity; for me a retiring place to write a book and spring more effectively back into the maelstrom. Strange that the same habitat should prove favourable to ambitions so glaringly opposed.

Conventual High Mass was at ten every morning, immediately after Tierce. The beginning of this office was austere enough: the same silent entry of the monks, the same taking up of positions in the stalls that I had seen the first day at Vespers. At a tap from the Abbot, the monks stooped almost double in silent prayer, their rows of tonsures appearing for a minute on either side of the aisle like tiers of discs. (Their heads were shaved once a fortnight. One day their scalps were as blue and overgrown as bur-

glars' jowls; the next freshly pollarded and gleaming in
their circles of hair.) All the canonical hours began in the
same way: "*Deus in adjutorium*," the hebdomadary monk's
voice sang on one note, "*intende.*" "*Domine*," the rest intoned in unison, "*ad adjuvandum me festina.*" A hymn
followed, one of those short poems with four-line verses
in the Latin of the Early Church, sung to an unseizable
little tune. Then, sitting back in their stalls, the monks
chanted the morning psalms in antiphony, the Gregorian
music booming from opposite sides of the chapel as each
verse of St. Jerome's Latin succeeded its forerunner. Tierce
ended, the officiating monk entered in his vestments, and
the deacon and sub-deacon, the acolytes and torch-bearers.
They genuflected together, and the Mass began. Every
moment the ceremony gained in splendour. If it was the
feast of a great saint, the enthroned abbot was arrayed
by his myrmidons in the pontificalia. A gold mitre was
placed on his head, and the gloved hand that held the crosier was jewelled at the point of the stigma and on the
third finger the great ring sparkled over the fabric. The
thurifer approached the celebrant and a column of in-
cense climbed into the air, growing and spreading like an
elm-tree of smoke across the shafts of sunlight. The
chanting became steadily more complex, led by a choir of
monks who stood in the middle of the aisle, their voices
limning chants that the black Gregorian block-notes,
with their comet-like tails and Moorish-looking ara-
besques, wove and rewove across the threads of the antique

31

four-line clef on the pages of their graduals. Then, with a
quiet solemnity, the monks streamed into the cloister in
the wake of a jewelled cross. Slowly they proceeded
through the cylinders of gold into which the Gothic tracery cut the sunlight. Their footfalls made no noise and
only the ring of the crosier's butt on the flags and the
clanging of the censer could be heard across the Gregorian. The procession reached the shadow-side, pausing
a few minutes while the sixty voices sailed out over the
tree-tops; and then back through the church door, where
arcs and parentheses of smoke from the burning gums, after the sunlit quadrangle, deepened the vaulted shadows.
The antiphonal singing from the stalls continued to build
its invisible architecture of music: a scaffolding that sent
columns of plain-song soaring upwards, to be completed
by an anthem from the choir that roofed it like a canopy.
The anthem was followed by a long stillness which
seemed to be scooped out of the very heart of sound.
After long minutes, a small bell rang and then the great
bell from the tower which told of the rites that were being
celebrated and the mysterious events taking place; and the
heads of the monks fell as if one blow had scythed them
away. Next, an unwinding, a decrescendo. The Mass sang
itself out, the kiss of peace passed like a whispered message down the stalls, the officiating court dispersed, and
the vestments were removed. A monk extinguished the
candles, the hoods went up, the Abbot intoned the open-

ing verse of Sext and, still on the same note, the response came booming back. . . .

Since the collapse and spoliation of the great Gothic church, its purpose has been fulfilled by the seventeenth-century chapter-house. Here nothing breaks the simplicity of white stone vaults and walls, nothing but the altar, a tall crucifix, the carved wooden stalls and the emblazoned throne of the Abbot. This severity gives immense emphasis to the splendour of the Mass and the austerity of the offices between which it is bracketed; but the lowness of the vaults is said to impair the effects of the Gregorian plain-song for which the Abbey is famous. St. Wandrille's only competitor is the Abbey of Solesmes in the west of France. Differences of opinion over certain musical details divide plain-song in France into two schools, each of which has its partisans. Both abbeys are famous not only for the magnificence of their liturgy, but for its purity, and for the care with which all seventeenth- and eighteenth-century corruptions have been weeded out, so that in neither ritual is there anything that does not belong to the Church's golden age.

———

Time passes in a monastery with disconcerting speed. Except for the great feasts of the church, there are no landmarks to divide it up except the cycle of the seasons;

and I found that days, and soon weeks, were passing almost unperceived. The speed of this temporal lapse is a phenomenon that every monk notices: six months, a year, fifteen years, a lifetime, are soon over; and, as I found it easier to talk to them, the only regret I heard was that they had delayed so long in the world before coming to the Abbey. They came from very different backgrounds, many of them very young after finishing their *lycée* or university course or after growing up on farms, others after years in business, as teachers, or as soldiers or sailors, officers in the Navy or the Merchant Service. They were recruited from widely different income groups; some had been married and widowed. The possibility of withdrawal during the long years of novitiate is constantly kept before their eyes, with the result that all who take their final vows are deeply convinced of their vocation. Finally, they become either choir-monks or lay-brothers, the latter position being originally calculated to give postulants, whose education or temperament unfits them for the studies that the priesthood demands, the opportunity of sharing the monastic life. Lay-brothers do not receive the tonsure, but wear their hair cropped close to the head, as do the novices, and are concerned mainly with the farm-life of their foundation, the fields and the cattle. As all the monasteries of France are unendowed, they have to keep going by their own efforts: every monastery has a subsidiary and purely lay function, which involves very hard work besides its other duties and one in which all must participate. St. Wandrille manages to keep afloat by the manufacture and sale of boot-polish and *encaustiques* for cleaning machinery, and by running a printing press. I asked one of the monks how he could sum up, in a couple of words, his way of life. He paused a moment and said, "Have you ever been in love?" I said, "Yes." A large Fernandel smile spread across his face. "Eh bien," he said, "c'est exactement pareil..."

———

The Abbot's table, on its little platform at the end of the refectory, was shared by a second figure whose ring and pectoral cross distinguished him from the other monks. Dom Walser was his name—the former superior of the Abbey of Beuron, in the Hohenzollern region of southern Germany, a large foundation housing several hundred monks. He had had the singular distinction of quarrelling with Hitler and the Nazi régime immediately after their accession to power in 1933. He refused to participate in the plebiscite, preached sermons against the dictatorship, and was expelled from Germany at the end of the same year, finding refuge at last in St. Wandrille, where he finally took French citizenship. During the war he visited America, served as a chaplain in the American Army, made frequent broadcasts to German troops, and opened a seminary for priests among German prisoners of war in North Africa: a tall, florid, bony, blue-eyed man, discoursing, behind the typewriter in his cell, with humour, gentleness, perception and, very occasionally, anger, about the politics and the movement of ideas in modern Europe. It was difficult to believe that he had been a monk for over forty years.

The uniquely visual relationship to which the quiet custom of the Abbey at first limited my contact with the monks, compelled me again and again to seek my parallels in painting; and Philippe de Champaigne, I decided, would have been the perfect delineator of the Abbot himself. Le Révérendissime Père Abbé, Dom Gabriel Gontard, possesses all the dignity, serenity and *allure* of a seventeenth-century ecclesiastical prince. My first clear impression of the Abbot, after the initial meeting in the refectory, was of him enthroned in the chapter-house, with a stole over his black habit, crosier in hand, and mitred. His tonsured flock lined three sides of an expanse of floor, in the middle of which two young men in plain clothes, one of them recently returned from Indo-China, lay prostrate, their foreheads against the marble. "*Quid petites?*" the Abbot asked. "*Misericordiam Dei et vestram confraternitatem,*" came the answer. "*Surgite in nomine Domini.*" The two young men rose to a kneeling position. It was a *prise d'habit*: two novices taking their first vows. Their tweed jackets were removed, the novice-master invested them in the black robes then slipped the scapulars over their heads. The ease, the gravity and the exquisite French of the homily that followed, the occasional citations from Latin, gave me a sudden understanding of what it must have been to listen to Bossuet or Fénélon—especially the latter, in exile in the diocese where he ended his life; Bossuet was too grandiloquent for the quiet tenour of this discourse—"Rien ne change dans la vie monastique," he said towards the end. "Chaque jour est pareil à l'autre, chaque année comme celle qui la précédait, et ainsi jusqu' à la mort. . . ."

When an abbot dies, his successor is elected by the choir-monks. His authority is absolute and lasts till his death. He and his monks are exempt from the authority of the local prelates and fall directly under the Holy See, where a representative of the entire order has a permanent position in the Curia Romana. An abbot's office is thus one of the highest importance. He is individually responsible for the temporal and spiritual weal of his community, for its discipline and economy, and for its contact with the remainder of the church and the outside world. It was a relief, after all these considerations, to find that the superior of my Abbey was an accessible man. He had a gentle, rather diffident charm that kindled easily into eagerness over the subjects that interested him—theology, the inviolability of primitive ritual, architecture, the arts, mysticism, archæology and history. He is a famous scholar in the monastic world, and I remember with acute pleasure our walks under the chestnut trees among the ruins of the old Abbey church, and the quiet voice at my side expounding, with such lucidity, the nature of Grace, the intricacies of Aquinas and Bonaventura or the ontological and moral values of good and evil; I can still see the charming smile, the donnish virtuosity, with which conflicting exegeses were confronted, demolished or reconciled. Often, as though it were a quite normal procedure, his voice would slide off *ex tempore* into the soft ecclesiastical Latin of the Vatican; and this easy breathing back to life of a language so long dead gave me, each time it occurred, the same spasm of delight. There were other conversations in his large panelled room, or searches in the library for some heraldic or historical detail connected with the early days of the Abbey—pleasant hours that a bell curtailed, when I would hurry off to the refectory, past the cell where I went to collect my letters each morning from the prior who was invariably reading the Old Testament from a large tome in Hebrew. Early in my stay I commented on the blessed relief from talk during so much of the day. "Oui," the Abbot said, "c'est une chose merveilleuse. Dans le monde hors de nos murs, on fait un grand abus de la parole." I had been living in dread of an event which would have turned this restful place into an awkward, even an intolerable sojourn—direct enquiry about my own spiritual convictions. But as the days passed, and no uneasy encounter occurred, I saw that the danger was non-existent; and I felt a fresh access of respect and gratitude to my hosts for their unconditional acceptance of a possible giaour in their midst, for their good manners and their charitable discretion.

Weeks passed, and the flawless weather of late summer melted into a clear, dry autumn. I spent much of my limitless leisure walking in the country round the Abbey. The forested hills of the demesne are cut up into long zig-zag rides, tunnels of beech that converge upon moss-covered urns supported by a single Doric pillar. Occasionally an archway appeared, carved with the Abbey's fleur-de-lis and, in one of the alley-ways, a shallow alcove had been hewn out of the rock, carved in segments and painted with the just-decipherable signs of the Zodiac, to form a sort of giant sundial. Fallen leaves now muffled every footfall, and the smoke of bonfires rose through the moulting branches. Lost in the higher woods, the oratory of St. Saturnine—solid, stocky and Carlovingian—suddenly arose; and, as I looked out over the descending tree-tops, I could see the Abbey buildings clustered like a city in the background of a tapestry. The rivulet of the Fontanelle flowed under bridges where the trout hovered motionless for hours in the cress-flowered stream which meandered away through water-meadows towards the Seine. Beyond, the grey buildings rose—the tall Norman refectory, the Duke de Stacpoole's fanciful arches, the Gothic quadrangular well of the cloisters, the high stone girdle of the Abbey pierced by the Abbé de Jarente's great doorway, scalloped and rococo. Then came the seventeenth- and eighteenth-century buildings, enclosing graceful staircases and wrought-iron balusters, crowned by triangular pediments whence scrolls overflowed, and symbols and flourishes; mansard roofs and a regiment of tall chimneys with their slanting smoke-plumes. Above them rose a grey belfry that scattered a little flurried cloud of jackdaws in the air with each initial chime. The ruins of the Abbey church dominated everything: clustered piers—fifteen or twenty stalks of stone gathered in vast climbing sheaves—branched into broken segments of aisle and chancel-arches, a few pillars of the triforium ending in mid-air, a pillar or two of the clerestory.... Beyond, I saw the timber and thatch of the village, and the vanishing wooded contours that, across the valley, corresponded to my vantage point. All these woods, though my footsteps never startled anything larger than a squirrel, still teem with wild boar. As it declined, the sun beat the grey Norman stone into thin edifices of gold; and, when dusk had swallowed them up, the buildings of the monastery were pierced by many gleaming windows—oblong and classical, Norman and rounded, or high tangles of Gothic tracery—as the Abbey prepared itself for the night.

Compline, the office that finishes the monastic day, belongs more than any of them to the world of the mediæval church. Only one lamp is lighted, enough for the monk who reads aloud from the *Rule of St. Benedict* or the *Imitation of Christ*. "*Fratres,*" a monk intones, "*sobrii estote et vigilate, quia adversarius vester diabolus tanquam leo rugiens circuit quærens quem devoret: cui resistite fortes in fide!*" The faces of the seated monks are hidden in their hoods, their heads are bowed; and they themselves are only just discernible under the accumulation of shadows. The solitary voice reading aloud seems to issue from an inner silence even greater than the silence that surrounds them. The reading comes to an end; the single light is extinguished; and the chanted psalms follow one another in total darkness. The whole service is a kind of precautionary exorcism of the terrors of the night, a warding-off of the powers of darkness, each word throwing up a barrier or shooting home a bolt against the prowling regions of the Evil One. "*Scapulis suis obumbrabit tibi,*" the voices sing; "*et sub pennis ejus sperabis.*"

"*Scuto circumdabit te veritas ejus; non timebis a timore nocturno,*

"*A sagitta volante in die, a negotio perambulante in tenebris ab incursu et daemonio meridiano.*"

One by one the keys turn in the wards, the portcullises fall, the invisible drawbridges touch the battlements...

> *Procul recedant somnia*
> *Et noctium phantasmata*
> *Hostemque nostrum comprime*
> *Ne polluantur corpora.*

The windows are barred against the lurking incubus, the pre-eighth-century iambic dimeters seal up any remaining loophole against the invasion of the hovering succubi. *Asperges me, Domine, hyssopo et mundabor, lavabis me et super nivem dealbabor.* After a long, silent prayer, the

41

monks were roused by a soft tap from the Abbot, and the rustle of their habits as they left the church was the last human sound, until, again in pitch darkness, they reassembled at four o'clock for Matins. As I left, kneeling figures of the monks, grouped like compass points about the centre formed at an angle of the cloister by a fourteenth-century stone Madonna of great beauty (half of whose face had been sliced away by the Huguenots), cast long shadows down the colonnades. From my window I watched the lights in their cells go out one by one, and then settled down, to fill the empty hours of the night, in front of the pile of manuscripts, maps of the Caribbean islands, photographs of Central-American jungle and of the blank faces of Maya Indians.

The Abbey had emptied of guests and I had been shifted into an enormous cell which might have accommodated a Cardinal or an Elector, the very setting for a huge four-poster and an arras representing Actæon being devoured by the hounds of Artemis. On the walls hung two sooty pictures—a near-Luini of St. Theresa, and a near-Murillo of the scourging of Christ. In the middle of the pink tiled floor stood a fluted Corinthian column of wood, which, three yards up, burst into a frilled capital, but supported nothing, as if it awaited a miniature stylite; part, no doubt, of some tremendous, now dismembered baldachino erected in de Stacpoole's day. The windows were uncurtained and there was nothing to hide the lovely shelving white planes that slanted through the thickness of the walls, and the ellipses of moulding at the top. It was a wonderful room to wake up in. Dreamless nights came to an end with no harder shock than that of a boat's keel grounding on a lake shore. Sunlight streamed in through the three tall windows and, as I lay in bed, all I could see was layer on ascending layer of chestnut leaves, like millions of spatulate superimposed green hands, and the crystalline sky of October framed by the thin reflected blue-white, or thick milk-white, or, where the sun struck, white-gold surfaces of the walls and window-arches and embrasures.

If my first days in the Abbey had been a period of depression, the unwinding process, after I had left, was ten times worse. The Abbey was at first a graveyard; the outer world seemed afterwards, by contrast, an inferno of noise and vulgarity entirely populated by bounders and sluts and crooks. This state of mind, I saw, was, perhaps, as false as my first reactions to monastic life; but the admission did nothing to decrease its unpleasantness. From the train which took me back to Paris, even the advertisements for Byrrh and Cinzano seen from the window, usually such jubilant emblems of freedom and escape, had acquired the impact of personal insults. The process of adaptation—in reverse—had painfully to begin again.

FROM SOLESMES TO
LA GRANDE TRAPPE

AFTER St. Wandrille, nothing in the routine of life at Solesmes proved unfamiliar. Its saga, from the time of its foundation in the eleventh century, was the same, on broad lines, as that of the first abbey I had visited. It had been an important rallying ground for the Crusades, from which a warrior had brought back the Holy Thorn still among the monastery's treasures; and in the aisle of the church lies the tomb of the Seigneur de Sablé who commanded the navy of Richard Cœur de Lion. Standing in the heart of the Maine, next to the Duchy of Anjou, it was in the centre of the debatable provinces of the Hundred Years War; and it underwent terrible devastation at English hands. The Huguenots, Commendation, and the Jacobins all did their work; and at the end of the Revolution, the priory of Solesmes was a ruined and empty shell. As they advanced, the armies of Napoleon emptied the monasteries of Europe; and, at the time of the Emperor's eclipse, the monastic idea was nearly dead. But, in the eighteen-thirties, a phœnix-like revival raised the Priory of St. Peter of Solesmes to an eminence only inferior to that of St. Benedict's own foundation at Monte

Cassino—a phenomenon due to the personality and drive of a single man: Dom Prosper Guéranger. This phenomenal monk rescued the ruins from the house-breakers, found backers who helped him to buy them, and established himself in their midst with three other monks. The community grew; the abbey walls rose; gaps were roofed over. Before he had reached his thirtieth year he was the abbot of a flourishing monastery, quelling revolts, quarrelling with his bishop, arguing with Cardinals, conversing lengthily with the Pope and, soon afterwards, purging the liturgy, publishing enormous volumes of theological commentary, corresponding, and presently falling out with, Montalembert, and founding monasteries in half-a-dozen countries. In the whole of Catholic Christendom, not a note of primitive church music can now be changed without the sanction of his abbey. His friendship with Villiers de l'Isle Adam persisted until the Abbot's death, and a brief but lively portrait of him remains in the pages of *Histoires Insolites*. His face, in photographs—bright-eyed, wilful, humorous, square-jawed—indicates his character as unerringly as the monastery that is his monument: a massive mid-nineteenth-century pile, its high towers and buttresses reflected in the Sarthe, and bearing, through half-closed eyes, the fantastical and exaggerated aspect of a Rhine castle drawn by Doré or Victor Hugo. When, during the Commune, the monks were evicted, they were sheltered by the villagers, and subsequently, little by little, they were able to re-instate themselves. The persecution of 1902 drove them to England, whence they returned after the First World War, leaving behind them, at Quarr in the Isle of Wight, a thriving daughter abbey. Dom Cozien, Guéranger's fourth successor, now presides in the ancient premises over a brotherhood of more than a hundred monks.

Much in Solesmes, and especially the refectory, reflects the Romantic movement. Here, among colossal pillars, baronial chimney-pieces and heavy Norse vaults, a slightly comic but entirely successful Romanticism prevails. It is a *décor* for Axel, for Corvo, for *Macbeth*, for an *Eve of St. Agnes* illustrated by Dante Gabriel Rossetti. The great chamber was further enlivened, during my stay, by the violet attributes, the portentous purpleship seated in the abbot's chair, of the ex-Archbishop of Aix-en-Provence. But the narrow height of the Gothic arches in the church are a convincing background for the splendour and complexity of the ritual, and for the perfection and volume of the Gregorian chanting. I stayed there two weeks, established in a warm cell, writing hard in front of a blazing log fire, enjoying the amenities of a library that must be one of the largest of any monastery, and walking beside the Sarthe through the quiet landscape of the Maine to the empty château of the Marquis de Juigné. An occasional companion on these outings was Father des Mazys, whose historical knowledge and skill in deciphering black-letter often took him to Juigné to study the archives of the castle, which are closely linked with the past of the

Abbey. I cannot think, without smiling, of the erudition, the volubility, the enthusiasm almost amounting to violence, of this splendid monk—a great-great-grandson of the Sir Hugh Macdonnell of Glengarry whose kilted, claymored and feather-bonneted lineaments Sir Henry Raeburn has preserved for us.

But Solesmes was a temporary halt on the journey to a far stranger monastery: La Grande Trappe, the fountain head of the Cistercian Order of the Strict Observance. My curiosity, which had been aroused by the reputation of this abbey, by the rôle it has played in French history and in the whole monastic life of the Church, has been strengthened by a fortuitous encounter with a young Englishman who had spent a year as a Trappist postulant. Shot down during the war in the bomber he was piloting, he had studied, after his release from a German prisoner-of-war camp, for the Anglican ministry. He had then gone over to Rome and plunged into the depths of a Trappist monastery. When we met he had just abandoned it for a Benedictine foundation, as the severity of the Trappist discipline had left him no time for study or solitude. I planned at once to leave for the Grande Trappe.

I set out from Le Mans, where, on a high rock above the steep roofs of the town, a slender Gothic cathedral is suspended in a spider's web of flying buttresses. An hour in Alençon, an afternoon in the market-place of Mortagne and a long crepuscular drive into the southern marches of Normandy were the stages of the journey which brought me, after dark and in drenching rain, to the village of Solignyla-la-Trappe. According to the Vercingetorix-whiskered peasants in the *bistro*, the Abbey was still several miles away, and, it seemed, of Kafkaesque inaccessibility. The butcher's van which at last transported me thither broke down twice in the middle of a moor. When the wind abated, we heard bells ringing through the down-pour. "L'Angélus," the butcher said, "les moines se cou-chent." An inky Gothic mass was soon perceptible and, a few moments later, the van had driven away, leaving me in front of an iron door. A one-eyed monk answered my ring and, after a friendly greeting, started off into the dark. As I followed him I could hear his clogs dragging on the flagstones and then making sucking noises in the mud. The Père Hôtelier gave me some food, and led me to a cell. His head was cropped except for a narrow hoop. His dress, too, was different from that of the Benedic-tines: a white full-sleeved habit with a black hood and a black scapular caught in at the middle with a broad brown belt. My cell was freezingly cold and, apart from a bust of Saint Bernard, quite bare. On a sheet of paper pinned to the wall were written in wavering script three columns of priestly attributes: poverty, humility, sacrifice, death to life—the catalogue enumerated a score. At the foot of the first column were the words: *Le prêtre est un homme dépouillé. Plus on est mort*, the second ended, *plus on a la vie. Le prêtre est un homme cricifié. Il faut devenir du bon pain*, said the third. *Le prêtre est un homme mangé.*

The Trappist Order, which is the loose and general term
for the Cistercian Order of the Strict Observance, is the
result of a series of religious and social revolutions. During the tenth century, about five hundred years after St.
Benedict's death, the group of abbeys centred on the great
Benedictine metropolis of Cluny was subjected to reform.
All accretions of laxity were purged from the observance
and the order was lifted again to the primitive heights of
asceticism laid down in the rule of St. Benedict. Soon,
however, the down-swing of decay ensued. Indolent ways
returned; the temper of asceticism was relaxed by scholarship and theological debate, and the Order was ripe once
more for a resurgence of austerity. The impulse came in
the twelfth century from the abbey of Cîteaux (from
whose Latin name the word "Cistercian" is derived), where
St. Bernard, the great Burgundian reformer, again brought
back the practice of his monks to the letter of St. Benedict's code, rescued a number of abbeys from sloth, and
set them climbing towards new heights of sanctity and
strictness. Today the spiritual descendants of these monks
are the Cistercian branch of the great Benedictine brotherhood. They remained on the heights for a couple of
centuries, but, in the fourteenth and fifteenth, they were
again sinking, and occasional reforms, all of them local
and sporadic, failed to halt their decline. By the seventeenth century, the evils of Commendation had under-

mined them, it appeared, beyond a chance of recovery. In urban districts the monks lived much as one sees them in Hogarth's picture of the Calais Gate; and the communities of the rural monasteries, dwindled by now to isolated handfuls of illiterate brothers camping in dilapidated monastic buildings, pursued the life of Hurons or of Iroquois. Their days were passed hunting with the local squires, oafish rustics with whom they also spent their evenings in eating and drinking heavily, retiring thereafter, as often as not, to the companionship of their mistresses.

La Grande Trappe was a fair example of one of these derelict monastic kraals. How it became the anvil on which the Cistercian order was beaten into new form, the almost legendary form in which it now exists, is a singular and fascinating story. The founder of the Abbey was a Count Rotrou III of Perche, Seigneur of Nogent-le-Rotrou, progenitor of the Nugent family of Ireland, a famous Crusader who fought the Moors in Spain and assisted at the capture of Jerusalem; and the foundation was intended partly as a thank-offering for his own safe passage across the English Channel, partly as a memorial to his wife, Princess Matilda, daughter of Henry I of England, who had perished in the loss of the *White Ship*. That disaster had made so deep an impression on him that he ordered the church to be built in the shape of a reversed sailing vessel, with masts for supporting pillars and an upturned keel as roof-tree; a shape that it retained until the French Revolution. The Abbey surveyed a desolate fen. The extensive lands bestowed by the Count were later augmented by King Henry II, in expiation of the murder of St. Thomas Becket. Centuries later, in 1630, it was conferred, with a dozen other benefices, upon an abbot who had never seen La Trappe and who, moreover, was only ten years old.

The early career of Armand-Jean le Bouthillier de Rancé was, for an aristocratic cleric in seventeenth-century France, remarkable but not abnormal. Richelieu was his godfather, and the Italianate endearments of Marie dei Medici while she dandled him on her knee were among his earliest memories. Rich, handsome, extravagant, and a favourite at court, he seemed certain of a scarlet hat. His studies at the Sorbonne, especially in Latin, Greek, Theology and Rhetoric, were brilliant, and, while still in his teens, he made a complete verse translation of the poems of Anacreon. When he consented, more as a dandiacal exploit than a religious duty, to deliver a sermon, his oratorical virtuosity dazzled the entire court. But his real preferences were for the poems of the Greek anthology, for fencing, hunting, clothes, jewels, lace, horses, equipages and the *monde*. It is not at all clear whether his passion for the Duchesse de Montbazon, a famous hostess and beauty over twice his age, was ever, in the full sense of the word, a *liaison*; but, whatever it was, the relationship is reported to have ended in the most macabre fashion. Madame de Montbazon fell ill. Rancé, entering her sick-room in Paris unannounced, discovered her decapitated body laid out in a coffin and, on the table, wrapped up in a blood-stained clout, the Duchess's severed head. According to the almost incredible rumours, it had been detached by a summary undertaker owing to the exiguity of the coffin. Pamphlets, gossip, and contemporary memoirs all conflict over details, but they concur in attributing the Abbé's conversion to a sudden confrontation with mortality in the shape of the Duchess's blood-stained cranium. Understandably, the shock was terrific. It changed Rancé's life. He sold his châteaux, distributed his entire fortune, resigned from all his ecclesiastical sinecures and eventually withdrew to his abbey at La Trappe, where he and his valet, the only servant he had kept, became monks. Clearing out the rebellious occupants and replacing them with a small band of practising Cistercians, he installed himself as their abbot, inaugurated a rule of the most ferocious austerity, and drove his willing flock back from the libertine era to the lonely and glacial mountain-tops of the sixth century—to the strict observance of every jot and tittle of St. Benedict's rule, and far beyond. There, with scarcely a concession, it has remained ever since. There the whole Cistercian order, except for some curious unreformed communities in Central Europe, is poised.

———

The programme of life in a Benedictine abbey had appeared at first forbidding; but compared with the Trappist horarium it is the mildest *villeggiatura*. A Trappist monk rises at one or two in the morning according to the season. Seven hours of his day are spent in church, singing the offices, kneeling or standing in silent meditation, often in the dark. The remainder of the day passes in field-labour of the most primitive and exhausting kind; in mental prayer and in sermons and readings from the Martyrology. Leisure and recreation are unheard of, and, in practice if not in theory, very little time is devoted to study. The diet consists almost entirely of roots; meat, eggs and fish are forbidden; and, over and above this austere regimen, a strict rule of fasting is enforced during six months of the year. At every season the monks are compelled to wear the same heavy clothing, a regulation almost unbearable in the rustic toils of midsummer. On summer evenings they retire after Compline at eight, and on winter evenings at seven, for a bare six hours' sleep. There are no cells. All, from the Abbot downwards, sleep in cubicles in a dormitory on palliasses of straw stretched out on bare planks. Heating does not exist and the monks lie down to sleep in their habits with their hoods pulled over their heads. Each Friday begins with a brief period— the length of two *Misereres*, more as a symbol than as a practical means of mortification—of self-flagellation on the bare shoulders with a *disciplina*, a monastic version of the cat-o'-nine tails. The weekly curriculum also contains an office known as Proclamation, a stricter version of the Benedictine *Coulpe*, or Chapter of Faults, in which the monks must publicly accuse themselves of minor external backslidings in observance or discipline. At Proclamation, however, Trappist monks are obliged to denounce each other, and to submit to such primitive penances as prolonged prostration in the cloisters or the refectory or being obliged to eat their meals on the floor. Except for certain officers in the hierarchy, the Abbot, for instance, the Cellarer and the Guest-Master, the rule of silence is absolute. A special deaf and dumb language for cases of necessity has been evolved and codified, and the entire lifetime of a lay-brother, who does not participate in the singing of the offices, may pass without the uttering of a word beyond the confessional or his spiritual consultations with the Abbot. A monk on the point of death is removed from his infirmary bed and laid across a bed of straw which is scattered over a cross of ashes. There, after the last ghostly comforts in the presence of the assembled monks, he expires. His body is exposed for a while in the church. No coffin is used at his burial; his face is covered by his hood, and he is lowered into his grave with his habit folded about him. His fellow monks, one by one, throw in the earth, and withdraw.

The Trappist life then, by any normal criterion, is sombre and stern. But legend, especially during the Romantic era, when it must have been an irresistible theme, has smothered its stark outlines with ivy-leaves of a still more baleful tinct. According to a rumour widespread in France, Trappist monks greet each other daily with the words: *Frère, il faut mourir,* and a mythical agendum in the duties of a monk is the digging of his own tomb, a few spadefuls a day. Another legend represents all Trappists as the authors of atrocious and undetected crimes, preferably the murder of their fathers and mothers, for which only the long penance of Trappist life can atone. Most sinister of all is the theory that the marshy country in which Cistercian monasteries are usually situated is chosen so that the vapours of the swamps may speed their inhabitants to an early grave. Even the name encourages such fables: the unwary traveller advances, the Trappe swings open, he drops into the dark, he is caught...

Many aspects of Trappist life lend additional verisimilitude. A few inches of a new grave, for instance, are always dug immediately after the burial of one of the community, and meditation among the wooden crosses of the cemetery is an integral part of the contemplative system of the Cistercians. Trappist abbeys are placed in flat landscapes because their monotony, like the repetitive dunes of the Thebaid, impels the mind to the contemplation of last things. (Benedictine abbeys, on the contrary, are nearly always built on hills. *Colles Benedictus, valles Bernardus amabat.*) Skulls and crossbones and other symbols of mortality were prominent in the past among the paraphernalia of Cistercian cloisters. Châteaubriand was unable to resist conjecturing whether the death's head on Rancé's desk was indeed, as it was rumoured, the skull of the decapitated Duchess, and a certain German-speaking

Trappist abbey in the last century was smothered with frescoes of the most alarming kind. Symbols of death and dissolution confronted the eye at every turn, and in the refectory the beckoning torso of a painted skeleton, equipped with an hour-glass and a scythe, leant, with the terrifying archness of a forgotten guest, across the coping of a wall on which were inscribed the words: Tonight, perhaps?* It is scarcely marvellous that the most liberal-minded laymen have detected in such disturbing symbolism, in the perpetual silence, the ghostly costume and the pervading melancholy of a Trappist abbey, no message but one of despair and a morose delectation of Death. To understand these Cistercian rigours, we must dismiss modern accommodations and rationalisations and seek to return to the uncompromising literalness of the early Christians. Prayer for the redemption of mankind is the basis of Benedictine monasticism; and in the Cistercian branch of the Benedictine family the principle of prayer has been supplemented by the idea of vicarious penance. The origins of this concept are to be found in the forty days and forty nights in the wilderness and, indeed, in the Crucifixion itself. Vicarious penance became the distinguishing spiritual exercise of the Cistercian order, and the reasons that led the monks of St. Bernard's time to mould their monasticism into its own distinctive shape have lost, for present-day Trappists, none of their impact.

---

*Heute Nacht, vielleicht?

The overwhelming sadness of a Trappe, therefore, is no fortuitous by-product of the Cistercian way of life but one of its vital preconditions. A Cistercian Cloister is a workshop of intercession and a bitter cactus-land of expiation for the mountains of sin which have accumulated since the Fall. A Trappist career is a long-drawn-out atonement, a protracted imitation of the Wilderness, the Passion, the Agony in the Garden, the Way of the Cross, and the final sacrifice of Golgotha. By fierce asceticism, cloistered incarceration, sleeping on straw and rising in the darkness after a few hours' sleep, by abstinence, fasting, humiliation, the hair shirt, the scourge, the extremes of heat and cold, and the unbroken cycle of contemplation, prayer and back-breaking toil,* they seek, by taking the sins of others on to their own shoulders, to lighten the burden of mankind. But, in spite of its rigours, this life of penance has certain spiritual consolations. A Cistercian writer describes them as the Triple Unction of the Soul. The first unction is the lightness, the spiritual buoyancy, the experience of liberty regained by the shedding of all earthly possessions and vanities and ambitions; and by aspiring to, and sometimes achieving, a life that is free from personal sin. This aspect of Cistercian life is prominent in Thomas Merton's book *Elected Silence*. The second is the joy that springs from the conviction that their prayers and

---

*One of the lay-brothers of Thimadeuc, in Brittany, finding these mortifications inadequate, is wont to fill his *sabots* with thorns before beginning the labours of the day.

penances unloose upon the world a healing flood of atonement which saves the souls and lightens the guilt of mankind. The third is the belief that this life of sacrifice is dedicated to God, that it derives from love of Him, and draws the soul closer to Him. Cistercian contemplation, so far as I can understand it, has little in common with the complex processes recorded in the writings of the great mystics; for a humble and completely unintellectual simplicity is one of the characteristics of the Trappist order. Their contemplative system consists mainly of the dedication of every action, and of every second, to God. With time and practice, this permanent concentration of the mind upon God brings a full reward: peace of the soul, a kind of divine ravishment, an unspeakable happiness that a French Trappist writer describes as a prolonged intimation of Paradise.

Plainly, vocations for the Cistercian order must be of no ordinary kind. There is much, in theory, to persuade an intellectual convert to plunge headlong into a Trappe; but in practice, as had happened to my ex-Trappist friend, there is also much to repel him. It is not the asceticism, the hardships and the toil so much as the general rawness of the life and the fact that the offices of the church and the labour in the fields leave so little time for study and meditation. The *beata solitudo* of the Cistercians must refer to the remoteness of the abbeys, their deserted surroundings and the personal solitude which is attained through the rule of silence; for, in fact, a Trappist is seldom alone. He has no cell to which he can retire, and even his hours of study (so often encroached upon by the other demands of the monastery life), are spent, exhausted with toil, at a communal desk in the scriptorium. One may search in vain among the Cistercians for the magnificent libraries that are one of the glories of the cultivated Benedictine order: those great treasure houses like Monte Cassino and Cluny and St. Germain and St. Gall, where all the learning and wisdom of the world outside the walls of Byzantium was stored through the Middle Ages.

It may be an exaggeration to say—as has at times been said—that a Trappist must augment his triple vow of poverty, obedience and chastity by a further vow of ignorance. But it is certain that Rancé, after becoming Abbot of the Grande Trappe, was a declared enemy of the learning, philosophy and theological speculation which play so large a part in Benedictine life. The more closely one studies him, how antipathetic Rancé appears! His biography by the Abbé Brémond* is, admittedly, hostile; but not even Châteaubriand's romantic encomium** can disguise the dominating bigotry and, sometimes, cruelty of his later character; his suppression of learning; his long and venomous controversy upon this very issue of monastic scholarship with Father Mabillon, the great Benedictine savant of Saint-Germain-des-Prés; his perversion of

---

* *L'Abbé Tonnerre.*
** *Vie de Rancé* and *Mémoires d'Outre-tombe.*

the stern Cistercian Rule into a régime of unbearable harshness; the constant spying on his monks; his merciless intolerance of physical debility; his savage punishments; and, worst of all, his system of testing the monastic discipline by accusations of faults that had never been committed. He developed into an atrocious bully, restless, quarrelsome, vindictive, domineering and, under a simulacrum of humanity, proud—all, in fact, that a Cistercian should not be. The brocaded libertine of his early days remains easily the more likeable of his two personalities. He was, nevertheless, a great reformer, who saved the Cistercian Order from decay and, perhaps, from dissolution. The sagacious abbots of later times brought the rule of the abbey back to the injunctions of St. Benedict and St. Bernard, which, by any normal standards, are exacting enough.

———

I thanked my good fortune, during the next few days, for my chance meeting with the ex-Trappist, since, at the Trappe, there was no contact with the monks. I ate my meals alone in the guest-house, listening over a loud-speaker to the reading in the refectory, and whiled away the rest of my time alone in my cell or wandering about the demesne. In church there was a kind of minstrels' gallery from which the guests, like Moslem ladies in a zenana, gazed down at the Trappists. The Victorian

Gothic architecture of the church had none of the Romantic splendour of Solesmes; it was a great, dark north-Oxford nightmare, a grey sepulchre in the depths of which, hour upon hour, the chanting monks stood or knelt. The glaucous light was drained of colour. Fathoms below, columns of beard and brown home-spun, were the fore-shortened lay-brothers. Beyond, their white habits and black scapulars covered by voluminous cowls, evolved the choir-monks. Each topiaried head was poised, as it were, on three cylinders of white fog: the enveloped body flanked by two sleeves so elongated and tubular that their mouths touched the ground, flipping and swinging, when the monks were in motion, like the ends of elephants' trunks. From the vestments to the wooden candle-sticks and the wooden crosier of the Abbot, all was rigorously simple, and very different were the offices from the magnificent singing and the coruscating ritual of St. Wandrille and Solesmes. There was something immensely impressive, nevertheless, about these interminable periods in the dark, by the light of candle-flames or in the watery pallor of the mid-morning, of alternate chanting and silence, the rows of monks behind the iron-studded breviaries a yard square, and the stiff and illuminated pages all turning together as the hours of liturgy wore on; the slow processions and the hooded figures kneeling on the stone. Often, in the morning, the Conventual High Mass was replaced by the Office of the Dead and the cheerless ogival masonry of the church was stirred by the slow thunder of the *Dies Irae*. The most uplifting moment was the long majestic chanting of the *Salve Regina* at the end of Compline. Cistercians are under the especial aegis of the Blessed Virgin and an office is devoted to her which is absent from the liturgy of other monastic orders, as though this element of maternal gentleness were somehow indispensable in the perennial hardship of their life.

In the daylight that followed my arrival, the pale grey Trappe resembled not so much an abbey as a hospital, an asylum or a reformatory. It dwindled off into farm buildings, and came to an end in the fields where thousands of turnips led their secret lives and reared into the air their little frostbitten banners. Among the furrows an image mouldered on its pedestal; and, under a sky of clouded steel, the rooks cawed and wheeled and settled. Across the December landscape, flat and waterlogged with its clumps of drizzling coppice and barren-looking pasture-land, ran a rutted path which disappeared beneath an avenue of elm-trees. Willows, blurred and colourless as the detail of an aquatint, receded in the mist; and, here and there, the pallor of the woods was interrupted by funereal clumps of pine. Isolated monks, all of them hooded and clogged, at work in the fields, ploughing or chopping wood, dotted this sodden panorama and the report of their falling axes reached the ear long seconds after the visual impact. Others were driving slow herds of cattle to graze. Two of them would converse for a few seconds in their extraordinary semaphore, and then "Viens, la blanche!"

or, "à droite, grosse bête!" would break the silence as a cow or a laggard cart-horse was urged through a gap in a hedge.* Then the stillness fell once again, and an occasional sequence of gestures was the only discourse between mortals. All the revenues of Trappist foundations are derived from farming; and in the Middle Ages the Cistercians were the most famous and most extensive horse-breeders in Christendom. Trappist lay-brothers are predominantly of peasant origin and many of them are gigantic raw-boned men; horny handed, weather-beaten and muscular; for the austerity of the diet, the arduous labour and the lack of sleep have on the monks the reverse of a debilitating effect and seem to furnish them with almost indestructible health. (The lay-brothers wear habits of some coarse brown stuff like sacking and their heads are completely shaven and all of them are bearded. The whole community are shod in *sabots*. Between the lay-brothers and the white-clad, razored choir-monks with their thin circlets of hair, the contrast is extremely striking.) Later, when the air became brittle with frost and the puddles underfoot creaked with the first ice of winter, the country surrounding the Trappe was transformed into the world of Breughel and Hieronymus Bosch—their world, with some element even more Nordic and haggard and frightening which suggested Grünewald.

---

*There is a special dispensation from the rule of silence for the monks who deal with the abbey livestock when they are actually addressing their dumb charges.

Round the Trappe, edged by hazel and silver birch and teeming with water fowl, are scattered seven stagnant pools. The largest of these, l'Etang de Rancé, is only a furlong from the Abbey and the monks wander here during their periods of meditation, or sit among the reeds with their eyes downcast upon their breviaries or merely gazing across the water, on giant cement mushrooms. The woods are full of game no longer hunted. It is said that Rancé, remembering his early passion for the chase when his cell was invaded by the belling of the stags and the echo of the hounds and hunting horns, suffered moments of anguished longing for the world of his old pursuits. Clenching his teeth and covering his ears, he burned with all the fires of Ulysses bound to the mast among his wax-deafened oarsmen as they sailed past the siren-islands.

What happens, I had asked my ex-Trappist friend, when a monk is assaulted by temptation? He answered that he had experienced gruelling struggles with the flesh, battles that lasted for days, and from which he had barely emerged victorious. The mind was usually so occupied by the multitude of religious duties and the body by the brunt of labour, that months passed without a whisper. Then, all of a sudden, the siege of restless thoughts would begin. As often as not, profane and carnal visions would be reinforced by the murmurings of religious doubt, and at the end of these alarming onslaughts, from which he emerged unscathed only with the help of prayer and a kind of mental flight, he would feel utterly exhausted.

Flight was the best manœuvre; since, by remaining on the spot and answering the Devil blow for blow, he, an amateur in these combats, lay himself open to diabolical casuistry and the renewal, under Protean disguises, of a fresh series of temptations: weapons in the use of which the Evil One has had a million years to perfect himself. These ordeals were succeeded by a terrible prostration, but also by a feeling of victory, a conviction that the dragon, so to speak, had been killed for ever. When, after the first experience, he expressed this thought to his confessor, the wise old monk ruefully shook his head and assured him that no monk, however holy, could say that he was immune for life; the Devil, incensed by defeat, lulled his foe by inaction, and then returned to the attack with sevenfold reinforcements. The sole remedy lay in the strengthening of faith, the redoubling of austerities and in increased skill in these Parthian stratagems of the soul.

Of the triple cenobitic vow, that of chastity, it had always occurred to me, would, over a lifetime, be the most exacting. The primitive adjunct of hair-shirts, destined to promote a counter-irritant to the sting of concupiscence, has fallen almost completely into disuse—largely, a Benedictine told me with a smile, because they sometimes propagate, rather than diminish, the dangers they are destined to allay. Only spiritual and mental solutions remain. It seems tragic that a lifetime of ascesis effects no permanent mental extirpation equivalent to the physical extremes of Abelard and Origen and of the Skapetz of the Danube

Delta. Mental discipline, prayer and remoteness from the world and its disturbing visions reduce temptation to a minimum, but they can never entirely abolish it. In mediæval traditions, abbeys and convents were always considered to be inexpugnable centres of revolt against infernal dominion on earth. They became, accordingly, especial targets. Satan, issuing orders at nightfall to his foul precurrers, was rumoured to dispatch to capital cities only one junior fiend. This solitary demon, the legend continues, sleeps at his post. There is no work for him; the battle was long ago won. But monasteries, those scattered danger points, become the chief objectives of nocturnal flight; the sky fills with the beat of sable wings as phalanx after phalanx streams to the attack, and the darkness crepitates with the splintering of a myriad lances against the masonry of asceticism. Piety has always been singled out for the hardest onslaught of hellish aggression. The empty slopes of the wilderness became the lists for an unprecedented single combat, lasting forty days and nights, between the leaders of either faction; when the Thebaid filled up with hermits, their presence at once attracted a detachment of demons, and round the solitary pillar of St. Symeon the Stylite, the Powers of Darkness assembled and spun like swarming wasps.

What, a psychiatrist may ask, are the results of the manhandling of the delicate machinery of the psyche which these struggles involve? Can so many human instincts be seized like a handful of snakes, tied up in a sack, and locked away, alive and squirming, for a lifetime? There seems no possibility of getting an answer. If the principles of psychiatry are exact, these men must be Pandora's boxes that no amount of prayer or faith or will-power could save from eventual explosion; and the same theories, of course, turn the whole army of saints and martyrs with one blow of the pen into potential madmen. Yet nothing happens. There is no secular power that can hold a monk captive in his cloister; indeed, the anticleri-cal bias of many governments would consider every deser-tion as a blow against obscurantism and reactionary forces. But apostasy is very rare. A novice whose intellec-tual leanings are stronger than his ascetic bent may leave the strict discipline of a Cistercian abbey for the milder Benedictine régime; or he may, if he has mistaken his vo-cation, abandon the monastic life altogether. But defec-tion, after the long novitiate has ended and the final vows have been taken, very seldom occurs. French monasteries are barren ground for the supply of the weekly *chronique scandaleuse* with which unhappy members of the non-celibate clergy of other lands furnish so liberal a measure. There was not the faintest indication, my ex-Trappist friend told me, in any of the abbeys he had lived in, of homosexual activities, or even, as far as he could see, of homosexual velleities. The rare assaults of temptation, I divined, would present themselves in a more immediate and cerebral form. But this bottling-up of passions must escape somewhere: a Trappist cloister, I insisted, must boil with Browningesque soliloquies and stifled *Gr-r-r's*? Apparently not. Even the alien custom of *Proclamatio*, that terrible test of minor human frailty, leaves no scar behind it. All—and I profoundly believe this to be true—is quiet and peaceful, and the privacy of the individual silences is bridged by an authentic and brotherly love.

This psychological conundrum might be solved by an encounter of the champions of either side. A great mandarin of psychoanalysis should enter the arena with a cardinal expert in theology, dialectics and mysticism, who had graduated to the Sacred College from fifty years in a Cistercian monastery. Alas, the terms of reference of the antagonists would be so different and irreconcilable, so incapable of engaging, that the match might turn into a double exhibition of shadow-boxing: the psycho-analyst aiming murderous strokes with the repression of the libido, followed through by the Id, while the cardinal parried with the Action of Grace and the Paraclete, and drove his advantage home with Pseudo-Dionysios the Areopagite; leaving the opponents panting, unharming and unharmed, and crowd and umpire more bewildered than before. The secret of monastic life, that entire abdication of the will and the enthronement of the will of God which solves all problems and trials and turns a life of such acute outward suffering into one of peace and joy, is a thing that it is given to few outside a cloister fully to comprehend.

The dissimilarity, on closer contact, of the only three

monks to whom I spoke, from the abstract Cistercian figure of sepulchral sadness that outward appearances must have implanted in my mind, was a further source of perplexity. Each, within the scope of his function, was released from the rule of silence. The first was the Guest-Master, the young auburn-haired monk who was responsible for the part of the abbey where I lived: a young man of extreme good looks, great charm and a glance of the most disarming integrity and friendliness. He was surrounded by an aura of composure and peace rarely encountered among laymen. The second was the monk who showed me the monastery, the cloisters, the chapter-house, the various chapels, the scriptorium and the refectory with its neat, disheartening rows of metal platters and jugs and its cutlery of aluminium and wood; a quiet, erudite man—the son, I learnt, of a wealthy manufacturer in the north—who discoursed easily and knowledgeably, as might a junior professor at a university, about the history of the buildings.

With the Abbot, Dom Etienne, I had more opportunity of conversation, for we travelled back together by bus, through the rain of Normandy and the Ile de France, to Paris, which, much against his will, he was compelled to visit on Abbey business. Here again was a disconcertingly normal man, with no trace about him of the terrors of Rancé; direct, thick-set, fair-haired, rubicund, with humorous and startlingly blue eyes behind steel-rimmed spectacles. Everything in his face and the slight Breton accent of his voice revealed a thoughtful and sober alacrity, leavened occasionally by a quiet, deep laugh. He possessed a singular charm and, like the other monks, an indefinable air of benevolence and happiness. Like many of his monks, he had been called up at the outbreak of the war and, refusing a commission, had served as an infantry sergeant until he was taken prisoner at the fall of France, remaining a prisoner of war until the armistice permitted him to return to his abbey. I said goodnight to this dignified and completely unaffected man outside the doors of the Convent of Notre Dame de Cluny, behind the Gare Montparnasse; then headed, profoundly mystified, through the rainy streets towards the Hôtel de la Louisiane in the Rue de Seine.

———

"Quelle morne et sombre solitude!" wrote a French traveller in 1771, describing a visit to the Trappe. "Quel séjour épouvantable et noir! Où suis-je venu? Je ne remporterai d'ici que des tableaux désolants et de lugubres souvenirs." Huysmans, travelling back from the Trappe at Igny in the Haute Marne during the 'nineties*—alone in his carriage, frowning, bearded, chain-smoking under a wide-awake hat—was filled with very different thoughts. These

---

*Not one stone of it, after the battles of the First World War, was left standing on another.

abbeys were palaces of light and virtue and tranquillity! How, even for one day, would he manage to keep intact, in the mêlée of Paris, the brittle armour of peace with which the abbey had equipped him, the precious deposit of truth and faith, both subject to his own frailty, his own debility before the temptations of a world he had loved, and which he now despised, and, still more, feared? What was the use, he pondered, as the telegraph poles chased each other past the windows, of surrounding Paris with a system of forts, of defending its approaches with pill-boxes and casemates and barracks? What the capital needed was a network of these amazing institutions, a sanitary cordon of monasteries where the prayers of the monks would secure the town from harm without and from the Midianitish prowling of evil within; even, such as their supernatural force, from foreign invasion. . . .

Where, I wondered as I walked home, did I come between these two extremes? Certainly not on the side of the anonymous traveller. Yet the reactions of Huysmans were a long way from mine. I had not, like Huysmans (under the name of Durtal in *En Route*), visited the Grande Trappe for a "décrassage de l'âme" and, very naturally, had reaped few of Huysmans' benefits. A visitor at the Trappe is too far from the existence of the monks, too sequestered, to participate in their life or to form any definite opinion. My initial depression had evaporated after a day or two, and turned into a kind of masochistic enjoyment of the sad charm of the Trappe, of the absolute silence and solitude; and my mood became calm and quiet and smoothed out. I had enough of the contemporary bias to experience a recoil from some aspects of the Cistercian order, and enough humility and *flair*, enough evidence that an almost superhuman generosity and unselfishness underlay the Trappist life, to know that both my recoil and my *flair* were inexact: that I was not in possession of any mental instrument with which to gauge and record my findings. I knew that, even endowed with an abundant gift of faith and with the monastic temperament, I could never become a Trappist. The Abbot of St. Wandrille, with whom I later discussed the mystery of the Cistercian vocation and life, merely observed: "C'est très spécial. Ça répond à certaines natures, mais elles sont très rares." This essay, therefore, must end in ambiguity. I am as perplexed and uncertain now as I was on that first evening after leaving the Grande Trappe when I approached the damp and smeared radiance of the Boulevard St. Germain; as unqualified still to deliver a verdict on the conditions and possibilities of life in that hushed and wintry solitude.

THE ROCK MONASTERIES
OF CAPPADOCIA

PASSING through Turkey some time after this expedition to the Trappe, I learnt that the remains of the old monastic community of Urgüb were only a few days' journey away. The site had been abandoned for centuries but, having always longed to see one of these desert monastic establishments of the Levant—so different from the convents of Western Europe but from which, after all, the whole of monasticism stems—I decided to see what it was like. The friend with whom I was travelling was equally eager for the journey, so, postponing a dozen alternative plans, we caught the train and set off.

Our three days of travel across Asia Minor, from Constantinople through Broussa and Ankara to the ancient Caesarea, was a journey backwards into a remote and dateless world. The lion-coloured uplands of Anatolia looked Biblical and gaunt. Buffalo-carts and an occasional string of camels, all heading for this odd town on the flank of an extinct volcano, raised long cylinders of dust, and thence our journey took us into the heart of Cappadocia. The plain and the crumbling biscuit-coloured villages, distinguished only by their minarets, fell away behind. The road wound into a stony cordillera then sank through a tormented ravine to the little derelict town of Urgüb. Half of it is hacked out of the mountain-side and appears about to subside again into its native rock, taking with it the threadbare acacias of the market-place and the circle of ancient and cloth-capped Turks bubbling in silence over their nargilehs—the last vestiges of humanity before the labyrinth swallowed us up.

For a labyrinth it was, cut through the soft tufa in deep gulleys that suddenly deposited us at the lip of a wide canyon. Curling into the distance, it contained within its steep walls a region of such wild strangeness that we rubbed our eyes—it was the landscape of a planet, the surface of the Moon or Mars or Saturn: a dead, ashen world, lit with the blinding pallor of a waste of asbestos, filled, not with craters and shell-holes, but with cones and pyramids and monoliths from fifty to a couple of hundred feet high, each one a rigid isosceles of white volcanic rock like the headgear of a procession of Spanish peni-tents during Passion Week. These petrified *cagoulards* extended for leagues to the farther end of the ravine, where they were reduced by distance to a barrier of sharks' teeth.

As our eyes adapted themselves to the glare, near the bases of the cones appeared minute dark apertures, ap-proached by rough flights of hewn steps. Descending into the ravine and climbing one of these staircases at random, we stooped through a dark portal. The steps ended in a glimmering chamber lit from above by a deadened shaft of sunlight. Slowly a Byzantine church, complex and tenebrous, materialised about us. We were standing beneath a central dome frescoed with Christ Pantocrator, his right hand raised in benediction; and all round, in the eight attendant cupolas, the shadows accumulated. Thick horse-shoe arches sprang from the supporting pillars, walls and arches being stuccoed and intricately decorated in ox-blood, yellow, pale blue and dark green tempera. Round the sides scenes from the life of Christ were frescoed, the Baptism near the start occurring in tartan-striped water which arbitrary perspective had reared into a tent-shaped cataract. The multicoloured evangelists, Solomon, fully robed and crowned, and Elijah splendidly mantled, glowered from the columns. Red rectangular seams across the floor achieved a simulacrum of paving. The illusion of an ordinary Byzantine church was complete.

The next cone contained a still more intricate shrine, poised high in the apex at the end of a dark uterine ascent. The church, richly painted with Betrayals and Last Suppers, had apse, dome and cupolas; it was flanked with aisles and completed by an iconostasis and a narthex; but—and so convincing was the imitation of a conventionally constructed church that it took some time for the oddity of it to sink in—three of the four pillars had been smashed clean away beneath the capitals. The survivor gave us the insecure feeling of children under a table miraculously poised on a solitary leg. The painted arches converged in three pendentives and hung there like stalactites. Only then did the freakish nature of these churches become fully apparent. Only then did we remember the vast, blind matrix of rock that pressed in on all sides, and into which tenth- and twelfth-century monks, outlining the doorways with adze and chisel on the blank rock face, had so astonishingly dug their warrens. What clearer proof could be found of Byzantine rigidity than the excavation, in defiance of every difficulty and architectural need, of such punctilious replicas? Not a detail was disregarded. Narthex and dome and pillar and apse and basilica were hacked out of the darkness as unfalteringly as brick was placed on sunlit brick by the ecclesiastical masons of Salonica and Byzantium.

The churches can be numbered in dozens, and the neighbouring hermitages by the score. Every second cone is chambered and honeycombed till it is as hollow sometimes from peak to base as a rotten tooth. Now and then the dark interiors are the size of small cathedrals. Occasionally, where the rock is thin, the brittle sides have fallen away to expose the painted prophets and seraphim to the open air. But most of them, posturing in stiff hieratic attitudes, are hidden in the cold, rupestral half-darkness: SS Constantine and Helen supporting the True Cross between them, St. John Prodromos bearing his haloed head in a charger, while an obliging curve in the foliage of a miniature tree redeems from scandal the nakedness of St. Onouphrios. The personage who appears most frequently

—for Cappadocia, in the time of the Emperor Diocletian, was his birthplace—is our own island-patron, St. George. Armoured, red-cloaked, heavily helmeted, and reproduced ad infinitum, he cranes from the saddle of his white charger to drive his lance through the serpentine coils of innumerable dragons. Eternal twilight surrounds these prancings and death-throes. But each time we emerged the same incandescent glare was beating down. Out of the shadowy churches, we were once more in the kingdom of *accidie*, in the land of the basilisk and the cockatrice, of Panic terror and the Noonday Devil. The day seemed stationary, as if Joshua, conjuring the cobalt sky, had commanded the sun to stand still.

Then, climbing a spur in the middle of a canyon, we peered into a deep valley, green with the foliage of plum trees and wild apple, overshadowing the winding track of a rivulet. The sides of the canyon, too, were covered with the straggling descendant of a vineyard: the last seedlings of vines and orchards planted here by the monks a millennium ago. (The pious Moslems of Cappadocia still drink a thin, pale brew—not unlike the vintages of Anjou and the Maine—in imitation of their Christian predecessors.) The wilderness was humanised. As we gazed, a flight of doves sailed out into the gulley with a sudden rustle, the sun catching all their wings simultaneously as they wheeled and settled in one of the dovecotes hewn for them by the vanished monks. They are the only survivors.

Who were these monks? When did they come, and

how did they live? Even Father Jerphanion, a scholarly Jesuit who studied this valley for twenty years, could find no explanation. Did they arrive as hermits in flight from the corruption of Byzantium and Antioch? The troglodytic refectories, with the long stone tables, the wine-vats and runnels scooped out of the rock, the great hearths still black with the smoke of those almost pre-historic meals, the shelves for kitchenware and the slots for hanging saucepans, all point to a communal life. Rows of trough-like tombs lie side by side in special burial caves. The date of the churches coincides almost exactly with the first irruption and early expansion of the Seldjuk Turks in Asia Minor. Cappadocia, in pagan times, was a famous refuge of the Zoroastrians. Did the Christians also seek sanctuary in these fastnesses in flight from the barbarian newcomers? These shaven-pated and pig-tailed hordes, leaving their gloomy Asian steppes, were sweeping westwards with scimitar and kettledrum on the first stages of the journey of destruction which was to carry them with the centuries to the walls of Vienna. While the Byzantine armies were contesting the Turkish advance, small wonder, then, if the Greek contemplatives of Asia Minor should have sought out such a place of hiding and seclusion. The vast stones, poised in grooves down which they could be slid to seal the entrances of some of the larger caves, would seem to corroborate this hypothesis.

For it is all guesswork; and a tentative reconstruction of the former life of the valley is more hazardous still. We can be certain that the monks followed the wise rule of St. Basil—the contemporary of Julian the Apostate, the correspondent of St. Gregory Nazianzen and of Origen—who had been born, centuries before, in nearby Caesarea. We know, too, that this was no hotbed of scholars and grammarians, for the iconographical spelling and the scrolls in the hands of the painted saints are arbitrary and phonetic. (Here, and in ejaculatory prayers hastily daubed in vermilion paint—"O Lord, save Michael thy Slave," for instance—the phonetic spelling provides additional proof that tenth-century Greek was pronounced exactly as it is in Athens today.) It was plainly monasticism of a simple kind. The Levant, at that time, was sprinkled with ascetic extremists. Anchorites immured themselves in caves. Stylites, seated on the capitals of ruined temples, wore their lives away in prayer and meditation, and the stranger Dendrites chained themselves for decades to the topmost branches of lofty trees. Perhaps the most likely analogy is to be found in Primitive paintings of the Thebaid in Italian galleries and in the ikons of the Orthodox Church—those toppling mountains riddled with caves and swarming with tiny dark-robed Fathers, all of them hooded or cylinder-hatted and equipped with voluminous and hoary beards and all busy at their individual tasks of praise and mortification and husbandry. One of them reclines on the spikes of a harrow, another wrestles with a demon, a third dreams on a pinnacle. Others plough, or pound their grain with pestle and mortar, prune their vineyards, or fish in streams with rod and line. Yet others are preaching to attentive congregations of birds, admonishing with lifted forefinger lions and docile panthers, or strolling by the banks of streams with their arms companionably clasped round the necks of antelopes and gazelles. The date of the valleys' evacuation is as problematical as that of the cutting of the first grotto, and as unknown as its cause. Contemporary chronicles and the records of travellers are strangely silent. One plays with the thought of lost edicts from Byzantium evoked by some unknown heresy, of a sudden berserk outbreak of the advancing Mongols, of decay through a falling-off of vocations; and then, reluctantly, for lack of evidence, every theory must be abandoned. The caves, the crepuscular churches and the numberless painted saints remain enigmatical as ever.

To a Western traveller's eye these relics lack the overpowering sadness of the monastic remains of Western Europe for several reasons. The uncertain date of their abandonment is too far back and, to all but the most learned philhellene and Byzantologist, the unfamiliarity of the Greek Orthodox liturgy and the Basilian cenobitic system that once quickened them give rise to quite different feelings to those promoted by ruins of a more familiar kind; and of these feelings, antiquarian speculation remains uppermost. Byzantium, from which the Eastern church derived its life-blood, has vanished, alas, forever, and the Christians that might have turned to these monasteries, had they survived, for refuge and inspiration, were swept out of Asia Minor decades ago, and today only Moslems inhabit these peculiar regions. The rock monasteries keep their secret almost as closely guarded as Stonehenge and seem as strange and remote to us as the ruins of Tintern or Glastonbury might to a traveller from the antipodes in a thousand years. Yet this valley of empty husks is the nearest thing in existence to the vanished colonies of the Thebaid in which all Christian monasticism has its roots. It was in just such a habitat—a world of tufa and dazzling sand that wracks the eyesight under the blazing sky of the Levant—that early Fathers like St. Paul and St. Anthony and St. Pachomius (who first gathered the scattered hermits under a single monastic roof) spent their arduous eremitical lives. This cruel and flaming territory is precisely the sort we must imagine as the background for the great St. Basil, for St. Gregory Nazianzen and St. Gregory of Nyssa, and it is in just such a burning wilderness that St. Jerome shared his Palestine cell with a lion and compiled the Vulgate. Thus, remote and unstirring and problematical as they may appear, these outlandish places are far closer to the primitive beginnings of monasticism than the dim northern silence and the claustral penumbra which the thought of monasteries most readily conjures up. The scenery of early Christendom lay all around us.

The sluggish sun moved down the heavens at last, stretching long shadows against the canyon walls. Leaving the cones behind us, we found ourselves in an empty region of cactuses and of iron-coloured tufa pinnacles balancing lumps of basalt on their thin and wavering spikes. A hushed and igneous land of hanging scoriae turning crimson in the setting sun. Suddenly we came to a well surrounded by Turkish women,—descendants, it may be, of the invaders who drove out the monks. On their heads their right hands supported heavy pitchers; and, at our approach, their left hands drew their veils across their faces with a fluttering and simultaneous motion. Then, in the shadow of a monolith, a rustic mosque appeared. So attuned were our eyes and our minds to the idea of excavation that the white cube, the dome and the minaret, it occurred to us, must be solid—or mysteriously embedded in some hard and transparent element through which we were magically advancing. The air was vitreous, intractable, crystalline. The whole world seemed inside-out.

POSTSCRIPT

NEARLY three years have passed since these journeys and the recording of them, and the Cistercian monks and the Cistercian life still seem as mutually irreconcilable, as mysterious and perplexing; and admiration and bewilderment remain uppermost in my memory. The ghostly monastic world of Cappadocia, too, remains as illuminating (and as irrelevant) as it appeared under the hot Anatolian sun. But later impressions of Benedictine life, perhaps because I have often returned to it, have been very different. Going back to my first haven at St. Wandrille (still on the rather strange and, it might seem, unsatisfactory terms of my first intrusion) and visits to Benedictine monasteries in England have robbed the Benedictine way of life of any feeling of strangeness. The changes of tempo involved in these sudden withdrawals, though they are still exacting periods, lack the violence of my first reactions at St. Wandrille; and custom has made the process of re-acclimatisation after leaving almost, though not quite, painless. But that first arcanum that a stranger penetrates after staying for a time in a monastery—the slow and cumulative spell of healing quietness—has lost none of its magic.

I am writing the last paragraphs of this book on the sill of a top-storey window in a Benedictine priory in Hampshire. The late afternoon is silent except for the sounds of birds in the leaves underneath and the sudden jerky movements of squirrels. The building, at this particular moment, is almost empty. Beyond the tops of the trees the October sunlight throws long shadows of haycocks up the sloping stubble-fields, and now and then it catches the steel of pitchforks as the monks of Farnborough toss the hay to their brothers knee-deep on the slowly moving truck. The roofs of houses and a further line of big trees mark the southern boundary of the monastic kingdom. Further still, a distant goods train stretches a long wavering ostrich feather of smoke through the elms. Not even the high anachronistic scream of a jet-propelled aeroplane, suddenly arching a thin track of vapour across the sky, can break the calm enchantment. And it is pleasant, after recording in earlier pages, as a kind of half-hearted devil's advocate, much that was amiss in periods of monastic decline, to gaze down at this small modern tributary of the ancient monastic river; a tributary very close in spirit to the crystalline limpidity of its earliest reaches, and which Western monasticism, after the many sandbanks and rapids and whirlpools involved in its long and winding course, has everywhere regained.

In surroundings like these the fate of the old monasteries which were once scattered all over England comes inevitably to mind once more and makes their disappearance seem doubly sad. Their names, those landmarks of a different and vanished world—ring in the ears in fortuitous and pleasant-sounding threes: Glastonbury, Tewkesbury and Gloucester; Sherborne, Much Wenlock and Fountains; Tintern, Montacute and Cleeve; Pershore, Abingdon and Lacock; Babington, Romsey and Ford; Littleshall, Valle Crucis and Maxstoke; Newstead, Abergavenny and Bolton; Welbeck, Canons Ashby and St. Michael's Mount. And how many more! England could ill afford their loss. But, though one may regret their passing, the small family of their spiritual descendants which has grown up in modern times offers us all that was most precious in the past. They began to reappear in England as soon as the relaxation of legal disabilities would allow, and there are now something under a thousand monks and about fifteen monastic foundations in England and Scotland and Wales.*

Cistercians are established in Pugin's abbey at Mount Saint Bernard in Leicestershire, at Caldey in Wales, and at Nunraw in Scotland; and Carthusians inhabit England's only active charterhouse at Parkminster in Sussex. Their origins are very diverse. Two of the great Benedictine abbeys of the English Congregation—Downside and

---

*These approximate figures refer to the male religious communities living in conventual enclosure, and should not be confused with the semi-conventual and secular orders which outnumber them many times over.

Ampleforth—had already existed for two centuries in exile before removing from Flanders to Somerset and from Lorraine to Yorkshire nearly a century and a half ago. The French—now largely English—community at Quarr in the Isle of Wight, emigrating from Solesmes as a result of the anticlerical legislation in France at the beginning of the century, followed exactly the same process in reverse. The other monasteries of the English Congregation are Douai in Berkshire; Fort Augustus—imposing conventual buildings gathered round the nucleus of a highland fortress presented to the Order by the Lovat family; Belmont in Herefordshire; and Ealing near London, which was founded from Downside in 1898. The Abbey of Ramsgate belongs to a branch of the Benedictine Order known as the Cassinese Congregation of Primitive Observance, from the stern outpost of which, at Pierre-qui-Vire, near Vezelay in France, Buckfast in Devon was also founded, and then built by the monks themselves on the site of pre-Conquest Benedictine and twelfth-century Cistercian remains. The story of Prinknash Abbey is certainly the strangest. In 1896, an Anglican community of monks settled in Caldey, a wild and often storm-bound island off the coast of Pembrokeshire, the haunt of puffins and guillemots and, formerly, of the Cornish chough. There, still within the fold of the Church of England and living in isolation and great hardship, they followed the Rule of St. Benedict, and finally, after seventeen years, the whole community, with the exception of two,* were received into the Church of Rome. After a short novitiate they took their vows as Benedictine monks and eventually became the founders of the Abbey of Prinknash in the Gloucestershire woods. They are allowed by the Pope, as a special privilege, to retain the white habits, instead of the customary Benedictine black, which they had first adopted as an Anglican brotherhood. Cistercians have now settled in the wild island of their origin. Prinknash has two dependent priories. One of them, a company of twelve, inhabits the half-ruined buildings of the thirteenth-century abbey of Pluscarden, near Elgin in the Highlands, where they took root four years ago. The other is Farnborough whose monks, till the arrival of the present community from Prinknash, were, like those of Quarr, originally drawn from Solesmes; and the part of the monastery in which I am lodged is built on the same massive,

---

*The two brothers who remained in the Church of England became the founders of Nashdom, which is one of the best known of the Anglican communities that follow the monastic way of life. These, and the many Anglican sisterhoods that wear the conventual habit and observe, with the greatest austerity, the Rules of St. Benedict, St. Augustine, St. Bernard and St. Francis of Assisi—even following, in some cases, the precepts of two post-Reformation saints of the Church of Rome, SS Vincent de Paul and Martin of Sales—are indications of the spiritual distance that has been travelled since the Reformation and the writing of *Areopagitica*. Some foundations are devoted to works of mercy, others pursue the contemplative life; one or two even observe the Cistercian vow of silence. The earliest of these Anglican sisterhoods, the Society of the Holy Trinity (now established at Ascot), was founded in 1845, at the height of the movement in the Church of England which is linked with the names of Pusey, Keble and Newman; and, nine years later, sisters from this community accompanied Florence Nightingale to the Crimea.

romanesque and neo-mediæval lines as that enormous pile. The priory church, however, is a fine flamboyant building. Gargoyles, crochets, finials and vanes adorn it at every point and it is crowned with a slightly anomalous dome that serves as a landmark across the surrounding fields. This was the inspiration of the foundress, the exiled and widowed Empress Eugénie, who lived the last years of her life in retirement near by. Three vast sarcophagi in the crypt mark the resting places of Napoleon III, of the Empress and of their son, the Prince Imperial, whose body was brought here after he was killed while serving as a British officer in the Zulu Wars.

A letter from a friend who is a monk at Pluscarden briefly describes his priory in the following words: "The monastery was founded in 1230 in one of the most beautiful places in Scotland. The church is still standing, without a roof, however; but one wing was restored and made habitable at the beginning of the last century. There is a small, exquisite chapel for which one of the brothers has made a wooden choir-screen and stalls which are worthy of the original. The chapter-house is a vaulted stone room with a central pillar and in one half of it there is a big open fireplace in which we keep a huge log-fire burning. The refectory is another vaulted stone room, very plain, with deal tables and whitewashed walls, and most beautiful. It is very cold and we have had snow constantly, but we manage to keep warm and I am really enjoying it. It is

certainly the most primitive monastic life I have ever
lived..."

It was the same friend who introduced me, many
months ago, to the earliest monastic letters in existence,
those of the great St. Basil of Caesarea. Living in the
fourth century, St. Basil was the first to change the
eremitical way of the desert into an organised cenobitic
life governed by a system of monastic laws; and it was on
his legislation that St. Benedict modelled his momentous
code a century and a half later. It is interesting, in view of
the aura of sadness with which many of its externals have
invested monasticism for the outside world, to turn back
to these early writings. "Light," "peace" and "happiness"
are the epithets, often recurring, that St. Basil finds most
fitting to capture the atmosphere of his cloister; and he
uses the words, not with the specialised and often threadbare meanings that they may have acquired in ecclesiastical apologetics and propaganda, but in the sense they
possessed in the literature of the ancient world. His long
letters, many of them addressed to his friend St. Gregory
Nazianzen, are leavened with charm and lightness and
humour. The polished Greek sentences are sprinkled with
classical allusions one would expect more readily in the
writings of a fifteenth-century humanist than in those of
a Doctor of the Church living in the reign of Julian. His
monastery was built on a flank of the Pontic mountains
overlooking the Euxine Sea, in surroundings that sound

very different from the fierce volcanic expanse of his native Cappadocia. "There indeed," he writes, "God showed me a position exactly fitting to my taste, so that I really beheld just such a place as I have often been wont in idle reverie to fashion in my imagination. There is a high mountain covered with a thick forest and watered on its northerly side by cool and translucent brooks. At its base is stretched out an evenly sloping plain, ever enriched by the moisture from the mountain. A forest of many-coloured and various trees—a spontaneous growth surrounding the place—acts almost as a hedge to close it in, so that even Calypso's isle, which Homer seems to admire beyond all others for its beauty, is insignificant compared to this." His letter ends with the words: ... "You will forgive me for hastening, as I do, to this place, for, after all, not even Alcmaeon, after he discovered the Echinades, could endure to wander more." There is a mood of humanity and simplicity in his writings, an absence of bigotry that seems to blow like a soft wind from those groves of olive and tamarind and lentisk; gently ruffling the surface of the mind and then leaving it quiet and still. And, while the daylight vanishes from these northern hayfields, it is a similar blessing, an ancient wisdom exorcising the memory of the conflict and bloodshed of the intervening centuries, that brings its message of tranquillity to quieten the mind and compose the spirit.

TITLES IN SERIES

For a complete list of titles, visit www.nyrb.com or write to:
Catalog Requests, NYRB, 435 Hudson Street, New York, NY 10014